Agile Testing Co

A Brief Introduction

Janet Gregory and Lisa Crispin

Agile Testing Condensed:

A Brief Introduction

Janet Gregory and Lisa Crispin

ISBN 978-1-9992205-1-8

Leanpub

This is a Leanpub book. Leanpub empowers authors and publishers with the Lean Publishing process. Lean Publishing is the act of publishing an in-progress ebook using lightweight tools and many iterations to get reader feedback, pivot until you have the right book and build traction once you do.

Contents

Acknowledgments

Our books always involve a community effort. Many thanks to our colleagues who contributed their visions of how the tester role is evolving in Chapter 11. We are going for a short book here, so we can't individually thank all the people from whom we keep learning new ideas and concepts to apply in our own work and transfer to more people, but please know that we are grateful.

More gratitude to the people who reviewed our draft manuscript and gave us such helpful feedback, including Mike Talks, Nikola Sporczyk, Lena Pejgan Wiberg, Pascal Stiefel, Barbara Zaleska, Bertold Kolics, Carol Vaage, and our copy editor Erica Hunter. Thanks so much to Constance Hermit for letting us use her wonderful drawings in Chapter 12, and Jenn Sinclair for her line drawings that we use so much.

A special thanks to José Diaz and Johanna Rothman for their lovely forewords.

And last but not least, we truly do appreciate our husbands, Jack Gregory and Bob Downing, who are always there with a glass of wine when we need one.

Foreword by José Díaz

CEO, Trendig.com

Life leads you to your goal. Who would have thought back in 2009 when I started the first Agile Testing Days (ATD) that I would write the foreword to a book by the Agile Testing Queens, even though Janet and Lisa have been part of the ATD ensemble ever since. I'm very happy and honored that they asked me to do so.

Agile Testing Condensed is in line with the two previous books of Janet and Lisa. This time they shed light into the corners and explore the edges of testing and quality in agile projects – short, concise, spot-on and right from the hearts of two women who dedicated their careers and life to share their knowledge and advance the activity of testing into an agile profession. It contains insightful examples and anecdotes and is fun to read. Both authors share their practical experiences and invite readers to retrace their journey through numerous projects. They take you by the hand for a walk through this challenging and beautiful world of agile testing and explain it to you. It is a treasure chest, for you and your team.

I recommend not only this inspiring book but also their true-to-work life training "Agile Testing for the Whole Team."

The book crowns their work of the last 20 years, in which they have dealt intensively with the agile world and its community. Their countless projects, trainings, workshops, keynotes, talks, webinars, lean coffees, coaching, open spaces, mentoring sessions, and conversations are condensed into this book and make its content so practical and worthwhile. This book is a must read for anyone considering a journey into the world of agile (including managers).

It is made for you and me. With a lot of love! Let's enjoy it!

Foreword by Johanna Rothman

Author of *Create Your Successful Agile Project*

You may have read Janet and Lisa's other books about agile testing. Those books are much more than just agile testing. I strongly recommend you read them.

This book, *Agile Testing Condensed,* focuses on how to create an environment in which the team - and especially the testers - can succeed. The book offers plenty of sources in books, articles, and blog posts that help reinforce the idea and offer you, the reader, ways to think about the issue.

Each chapter contains gems - that's the condensed part - that can help guide your thinking about testing and quality.

For example, too many teams think testing is about how a tester tests a specific feature. Instead, there's a section that helps everyone think about the product and how to plan the testing effort across the various levels of the product.

Another example is how they remind us about collaboration. From pairing to explore, to working in triads to define stories, testers collaborate.

I loved the section, "Testers are quality glue for a team." So true, and too few testers and teams take advantage of that glue.

If you're wondering about how to be an agile tester, or if you're not sure if you need testers on your agile team, read this book - a short and quick read that will pay dividends for a long time.

Why this book?

Our goal with this book was to create a small, concise, easy-to-read book that anyone could pick up to get a basic understanding on how to succeed with testing and build a quality culture in an agile context. Our first two (much larger) books go into more depth and feature real-life stories from practitioners. We refer to those books as:

- *Agile Testing,* which is *Agile Testing: A Practical Guide for Testers and Agile Teams,* 2009
- *More Agile Testing,* which is *More Agile Testing: Learning Journeys for the Whole Team,* 2014

This book is not an introductory testing book. There are many great resources available to learn the basics of testing, test automation, DevOps, and other topics. You can find some good links in our bibliography. Similarly, this is not a basic introduction to agile development. It is for readers who are on teams adopting agile or those who want to know how testing and quality fits into agile development and are looking for guidance, such as managers or executives.

How to read this book

You are welcome to start in any section, or read individual chapters based on what you want to learn. Each chapter is self-sufficient, although we may refer to other chapters.

Use it as a pocket guide to agile testing to keep handy as you work. When you get stuck and need inspiration, or when your team is wondering about a testing challenge, look through this book for ideas. When you want to get more in-depth, check out our other books.

Throughout the book, you'll find hints that will give you ideas about how to approach a specific problem.

SECTION 1: Foundations

In this first section, we share our definition of "agile testing." The heart of agile testing involves the whole team in testing and building quality into our product. There's a big mindset shift as the team learns to prevent defects rather than relying on testers as a safety net to catch them.

New agile teams learn to slice big features into small, incremental chunks and deliver small changes frequently. At the same time, they must keep the big picture in mind to maintain customer happiness.

- Chapter 1: What Do We Mean by Agile Testing?
- Chapter 2: Whole-Team Approach and Agile Testing Mindset
- Chapter 3: Test Planning in Agile Contexts

Chapter 1: What Do We Mean by Agile Testing?

Over the years we've been asked many times how to define "agile testing." We have included our "definition" of agile testing in the last part of this chapter, but there are many factors that go into that definition. Some of the practices that help support teams in their journey toward success are:

- Building quality in: teams focus on preventing misunderstandings about feature behavior as well as preventing defects in the code
- Guiding development with concrete examples: using practices like acceptance test-driven development (ATDD), behavior-driven development (BDD), or specification by example (SBE)
- Including testing activities such as having conversations to build shared understanding; asking questions to test ideas and assumptions; automating tests; performing exploratory testing; testing for quality attributes like performance, reliability, and security; and learning from production usage
- Using whole-team retrospectives and small experiments to continually improve testing and quality and find what works in their context

We'll elaborate on the above practices throughout this book. We do not consider them to be "best practices" because we know they are ever evolving.

Continuous testing models

Testing is an integral part of software development, along with coding, operations, understanding customer needs, and more. We like the models that represent a continuous or holistic testing approach. One of our favorites is the approach that Ellen Gottesdiener and Mary Gorman use in their book *Discover to Deliver*, 2012. Shown in Figure 1.1., the development process represents an infinite loop, confirming continuously – which is how we really develop software. We learn about a feature that our customers want, we build and deliver it, and then we learn how the customers actually use it. We use that feedback to decide what to build (or remove) next.

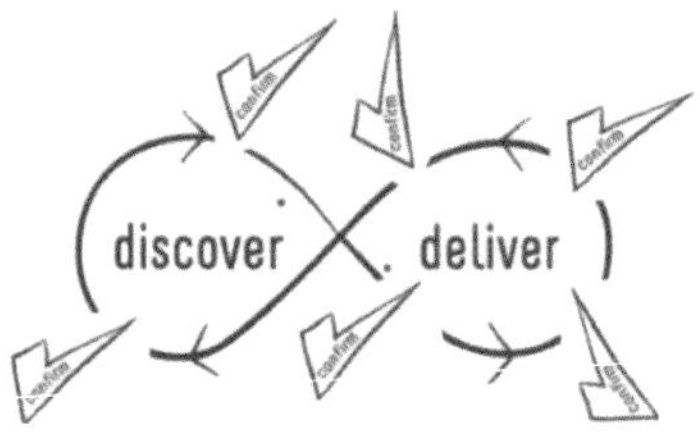

Figure 1.1: Discover to Deliver loop © 2015 by EBG Consulting

Dan Ashby took a similar approach using the diagram below (Figure 1.2) in his blog post as he talks about testing in DevOps[1]. This model shows that testing is an integral part of DevOps. We go into more detail on this subject in Chapter 8.

[1]https://danashby.co.uk/2016/10/19/continuous-testing-in-devops/

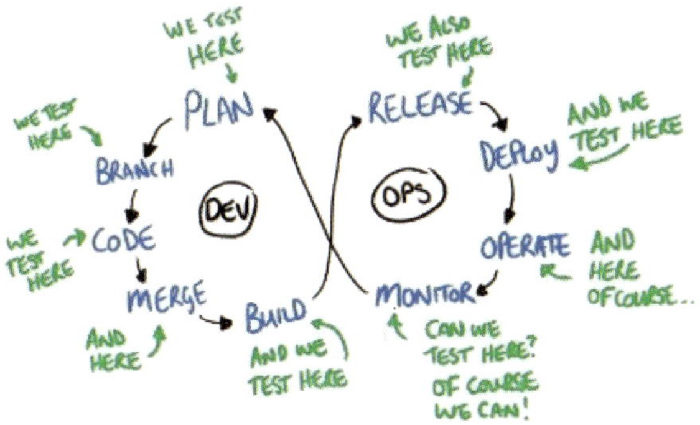

Figure 1.2: Continuous testing in the DevOps loop

We like terms like continuous testing or holistic testing and recognize that each team needs to adapt them for their own unique context.

Ten principles for agile testing

In *Agile Testing,* we introduced the idea of 10 Principles for Agile Testers. We realize now that these principles are not necessarily just for testers but for anyone in the team. We wrote these principles at a time when most testers were still part of a testing team with a phased and gated project, and the testing was at the end – after all the coding was "finished."

These principles still apply today for anyone on an agile team wanting to deliver the highest-quality product they can.

- Provide continuous feedback.
- Deliver value to the customer.
- Enable face-to-face communication.
- Have courage.
- Keep it simple.

- Practice continuous improvement.
- Respond to change.
- Self-organize.
- Focus on people.
- Enjoy!

Testing manifesto

We'll finish this chapter with this "testing manifesto[2]" created by Karen Greaves and Samantha Laing. Their manifesto reflects the mindset shift needed for a successful agile testing approach. We test throughout the development process, we focus on preventing bugs, we test much more than functionality, and the whole team takes responsibility for quality. You will find these principles reflected throughout all our books. Anytime your team is stuck on a quality or testing problem, reflect on these principles to find a way to move ahead. (Figure 1.3).

Figure 1.3: The testing manifesto

[2]http://www.growingagile.co.nz/2015/04/the-testing-manifesto/

Agile testing definition

The simplest definition that we've come up with for what we mean by agile testing is the following:

> *Collaborative testing practices that occur continuously, from inception to delivery and beyond, supporting frequent delivery of value for our customers. Testing activities focus on building quality into the product, using fast feedback loops to validate our understanding. The practices strengthen and support the idea of whole-team responsibility for quality.*

It takes a while to digest, and you can look at our blog post[3] for more details.

[3]https://agiletester.ca/ever-evolving-never-set-stone-definition-agile-testing/

Chapter 2: Whole-Team Approach and Agile Testing Mindset

Many software teams still use a phased-and-gated, linear approach to delivering software. People in a given role are siloed on specific teams, and they hand work off from one team to the next. The test or QA team is seen as responsible for ensuring quality, usually at the very end of the process and right before delivery to production, when it's too late to do much to improve quality.

In agile development, we break down the siloes and turn development into a continual, iterative process. The whole delivery team works together to build quality in throughout the process. By "whole team," we usually mean the delivery team – the people who are responsible for understanding what to build, building it, and delivering the final product to the customer.

Figure 2.1: A single team

In larger organizations, even those that have adopted agile principles and practices, there may be more than one team working on a product, such as an independent database team, user experience team, or other product team. In these cases, the whole-team definition extends to mean whoever you need to deliver the product. The DevOps movement has made the inclusion of operations in the delivery more visible. Janet refers to the people outside the delivery team as an extended family.

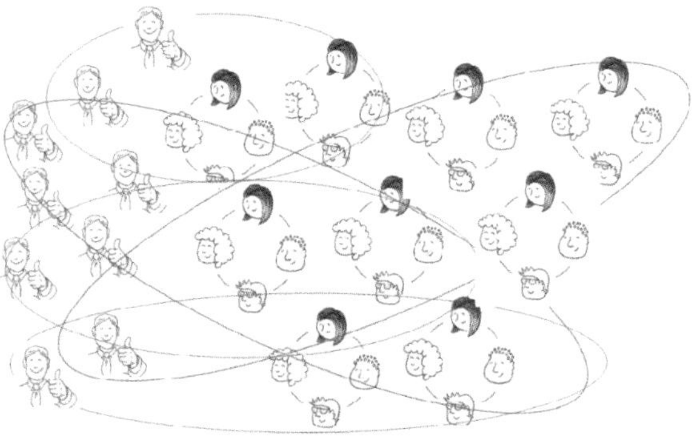

Figure 2.2: Multiple teams

Focus on quality

The whole-team approach means that all team members are responsible for the quality of their product. Part of this responsibility is ensuring that testing tasks are completed alongside the rest of the development tasks. When the goal is to deliver the highest quality possible, rather than deliver faster, the team builds a solid foundation of practices. To achieve that quality level, teams manage their workload so that they have time to learn core practices such as test-driven development (TDD) and exploratory testing. They also take time to learn the business domain and build relationships with business experts to identify features with the most business value and then implement them as simply as possible. Over time, by focusing on quality, teams do begin to be able to work faster.

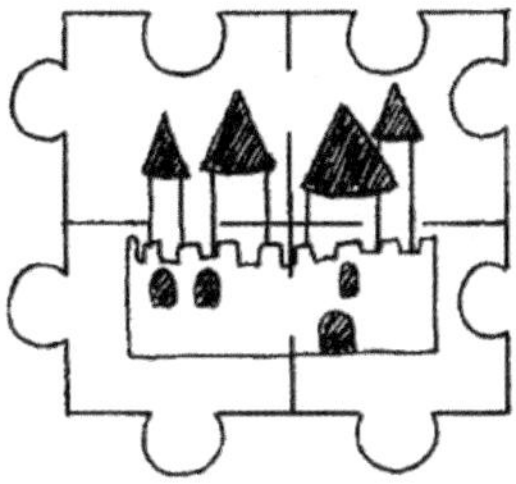

Figure 2.3: Your business value delivered as expected

There are several areas that require a change in how team members approach development. When the whole team is responsible for quality of the product as well as quality of the process, each team member needs to be proactive in solving problems. For example, everyone on the team can help figure out what is most valuable to customers. They work to deliver just enough of that value in small increments to learn how the customer uses that capability. By creating these quick feedback loops, the team can focus their testing on the features that are most valuable to the customer.

Each team needs to discuss and agree on a "valuable Definition of Done" (DoD). That should include how the team plans to deal with defects found in the code. DoD must include testing, and the question that needs to be asked is, "What types of testing do you mean?" In Chapter 9, we cover the agile testing quadrants and answer that question. DoD needs to be understood in the same way by every team member.

How teams deal with defects

One big mindset shift for testers is adopting a team approach to fixing defects. In *More Agile Testing*, we talk about focusing on preventing defects rather than finding them after coding is complete. When the whole team concentrates on building quality into the product by using practices like acceptance test-driven development and thinking about constraints around quality attributes, it can go a long way to reducing the number of defects found in the code.

Many teams practice zero defect tolerance. This means zero known defects escape an iteration or story completion. To make this work, teams must have fast feedback from testing activities so that any defects found can be fixed immediately. Once found, the programmers write one or more executable test(s), correct the code so the test(s) passes, and perform exploratory testing if needed. The team can then forget about it, knowing that they have corrected the issue.

Quite often, this philosophical change in approach helps to change an adversarial environment to a cooperative environment.

Multiple perspectives

Team members have different viewpoints, skill sets, and perspectives. We find that by using all perspectives, we have a better understanding of risks involved when delivering a feature. For example, designing for testability helps turn examples of desired and undesired software behavior into executable tests. Team members become generalized specialists – that is, they may be experts in one or two areas but are able to contribute to the team's common goals in a variety of ways.

Some examples:

- Testers may be experts at testing the product but can contribute to understanding the features and stories by asking questions to uncover hidden assumptions.
- Programmers can perform exploratory testing on their own code before checking in their code.

- Product owners execute acceptance tests on every story.

In Chapter 11, we'll talk a bit more about a tester's role and how it may change for agile teams.

Chapter 3: Test Planning in Agile Contexts

One of our top seven success factors from *Agile Testing* is "Don't Forget the Big Picture." Teams often get caught up in building, testing, and delivering the small increments – which we encourage – and forget about how that small slice fits into the system or how it works toward solving the business problem.

To plan testing activities effectively, a team needs to consider its context. To understand your context, think about three aspects of it: the team, the product, and the levels of detail of your system.

The team

Not all teams are created equal. If you're on a small, co-located team, you have an ideal situation for easy communication. You have a good chance of learning each other's values and sharing them. It's a sweet spot for delivering a great product, and planning is much easier. Teams can easily understand the next feature and dig down into story and task level planning.

However, many people work in large, globally distributed organizations. That brings on different challenges. Larger organizations have multiple projects and many teams. When they adopt agile, they often replace the silos based on role, such as developers and QA, with Scrum or feature team silos.

When many large teams work in the same code base, integration can become a huge challenge. Teams may need specialists such as performance, security, and reliability testers, but there may not be enough of them to go around to all the cross-functional teams. It's even hard to make all these issues and challenges visible. Release-level planning is particularly challenging in this environment but is critical to delivering new capabilities to customers.

No matter what the context, the delivery team must take responsibility for planning and completing all testing activities, even if it means bringing in specialists. If they have dependencies, they need to work with other teams to manage or eliminate those dependencies, preferably before coding starts. That said, adjustments need to be made to suit each unique context.

The product

The level of quality that your stakeholders want depends on your product as well as the type and amount of testing that might be required. For example, a content management system used only by internal users has different priorities than medical device software. Each has a different environment in which they dwell and involves different risks.

Consider the size of your product, how many people use it, or whether it is integrated with external applications. Think about how the product is delivered and the risk associated with the delivery mechanism. For example, if the organization is hosting its own web application, it has much more control about when and how often the product is updated. Or if the product needs to work on many devices such as phones, how do updates happen without interrupting regular usage?

One of the main purposes of testing is to identify and mitigate risks – to the user and to the business. Obviously, this plays a big part in how you plan your testing. This is one reason why delivery teams need to learn the business domain and work closely with business experts. Domain expertise helps when it comes to planning what to test. Does your team have a really good idea of how the product is used? Do all team members have domain knowledge? Collaborating with product and business experts helps the delivery team find optimal ways to build capabilities that your customers value.

There are many things to consider around your product domain. It is not only the software you are testing; it is the product that your end users depend on.

Planning across levels of detail

Testing across multiple levels (Figure 3.1) requires extra planning. Release cycles usually start by determining what might be delivered in the first "learning release." Perhaps only part of a feature will be delivered. Features are broken into stories and prioritized so the team knows which to deliver first. It's important that the team understands the big picture before they bring stories into an iteration. When developers work on a story, they're more focused on making sure individual tasks are completed. Testers sometimes fall into the trap of thinking only of the story they are testing, so reminders of the big picture are important.

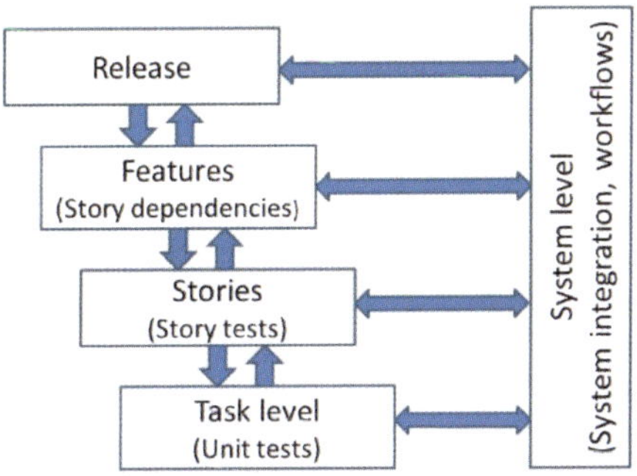

Figure 3.1: Levels of detail for planning

Release/feature level

Teams need to understand how each delivered story may affect the big picture, especially in larger or global organizations. Every release could be made up of many features, which in turn may be made up of many stories and tasks that have an impact on the system as a whole.

In large organizations with multiple teams all working on the same product, one of the problems we often see is that teams tend to become "siloed." They forget to talk to other teams to solve possible dependencies.

Figure 3.2 shows the importance of a test approach that includes all teams working toward a single product release. To give a big picture of test coverage, consider bringing people from different teams together to create a testing mind map or a feature test matrix (details in *More Agile Testing*) that encompasses the product.

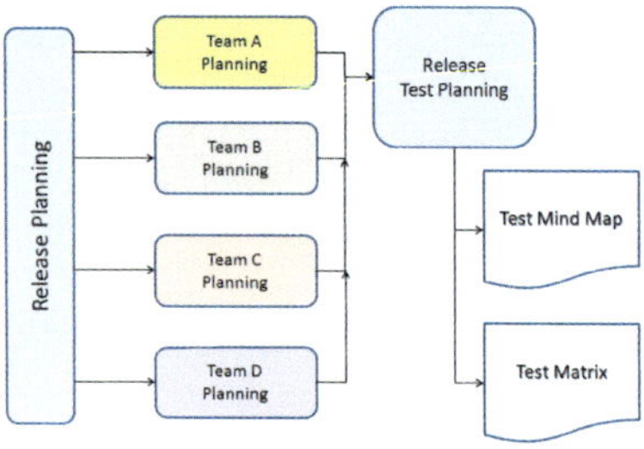

Figure 3.2: Planning for multiple teams

Remember, one size does not fit all, so make allowances for the size and number of your teams, where they are located, how work will be coordinated among teams, and whether all the skills needed for testing are available to each team.

Ideally, activities are coordinated with other teams as feature development progresses. However, it is important to note that a more finalized product may be needed for things like adding final screenshots to user or training documentation. Or, because it's not usually a quick process to deploy a patch for a mobile application, additional testing may be needed where the whole team explores the newest version one more time.

> ***Hint:*** *Do not make the mistake of having testers and perhaps operations staff wrapping up the pre-deploy endgame while developers start new stories. Just like development, preparing for delivery should be a whole-team effort.*

Story level

At this level, it doesn't matter whether teams are time-boxing their iterations or working in a flow-based method such as Kanban. Start with high-level acceptance tests (see Chapter 4: Guiding Development with Examples for details). Get examples to increase shared understanding of the story and turn those examples into tests. If the tests are written before coding happens, they help guide the development and prevent defects.

> ***Hint:*** *Consider what exploratory test charters might be needed (see Chapter 6). Think about the product's constraints and what that means for testing quality attributes (Chapter 7).*

As teams plan testing and discuss implementation for each story, details about testing emerge. Create new examples and tests to reflect what has been learned about the story.

Task level

Programmers use Test-Driven Development (TDD) to write low-level (unit) tests prior to each small piece of code. Some programmers call it Design-Driven Development since it helps them to design their code for testability. These tests are relatively easy to write, and they run quickly and give fast feedback to the team. They form much of the base of the test automation pyramid model we discuss in Chapter 10: Visualizing a Test Automation Strategy.

Planning for regression testing

Regression testing is about making sure the system does what it did yesterday. Contemporary practices for delivering small changes to production frequently leave no time for full manual regression checking, so the test automation is created as the product is developed. Test automation should be part of each story, especially at the service layer (see Chapter 10). If a story changes functionality, be sure to include tasks to change the existing tests.

Automated regression tests allow us to have confidence in our product with fast feedback. Many (if not all) of the tests run as part of continuous integration (CI). Some teams schedule slower tests to run less often. For example, running them several times a day instead of every build. Using release feature toggles to "hide" changes from production users allows teams to do some testing activities asynchronously as they continually deploy to production. The feature is "turned on" in production when all testing is completed (see Chapter 8: Testing in DevOps).

You'll find more information about this in Chapter 23: Testing and DevOps in *More Agile Testing*.

SECTION 2: Testing Approaches

In this section, we dive into core practices for agile testing. Using concrete examples to guide development is one of the most effective ways to build confidence in each new change. We share ways to help team members in different roles learn to collaborate to build quality into the product. Exploratory testing is another core confidence-building practice in which the whole team should engage.

Agile teams often fall into the trap of only testing for functionality – how each feature or capability should behave. There are many other important quality attributes that we need to test, which we also cover in this section.

DevOps and continuous delivery are hot topics today. We look at how testing and testers fit in and help their team succeed with those approaches.

Chapter 4: Guiding Development with Examples

The idea of using examples to guide development of features and stories has been used by many teams for years. We see it as a tried-and-true, valuable approach. Leading practitioners continue to find new ways to help teams succeed with these techniques: for example, Matt Wynne's example mapping (see more in Chapter 5).

Concrete examples of desired and undesired system behavior help teams build a shared understanding of each feature and story. This enables them to build the right thing with fewer story rejections and shorter cycle time from start to production deploy. Testers contribute by asking for these concrete examples and using them to create executable tests that guide development. They can be the voice of experience at leading these conversations.

Example-based methods

There are a few variations for building features and stories based on examples. Behavior-driven development (BDD) is the one that Janet hears most teams claim they use. BDD, first introduced by Daniel Terhorst-North, captures example scenarios in a natural, domain-specific language. The "Given/When/ Then" syntax describes preconditions, some trigger action, and resulting post-condition. As developers write the production code, they are likely to automate some or all the scenarios to help know when they've delivered what the customer wants.

Writing these scenarios may sound easy, but it takes practice to simplify tests so that there really is only one thing being tested. See Figure 4.1 for an example.

Acceptance test-driven development (ATDD) is similar. It is a more generic form of guiding development with examples without strict language or rules. Most people use ATDD for functional tests, although requirements for other quality attributes, such as security or accessibility, can be included. One ATDD approach we've used is to capture at least one high-level example of desired or "happy path" behavior and at least one example for each type of misbehavior as the team plans the story. Testers and other team members elicit more detailed examples as coding proceeds on the story. At least some of the examples are turned into executable tests that help the team decide when they're done.

Figure 4.1 shows a progression starting with slicing the feature into stories. The blue bubbles are done as part of story readiness workshops, backlog refinement, or "three amigos" discussions.

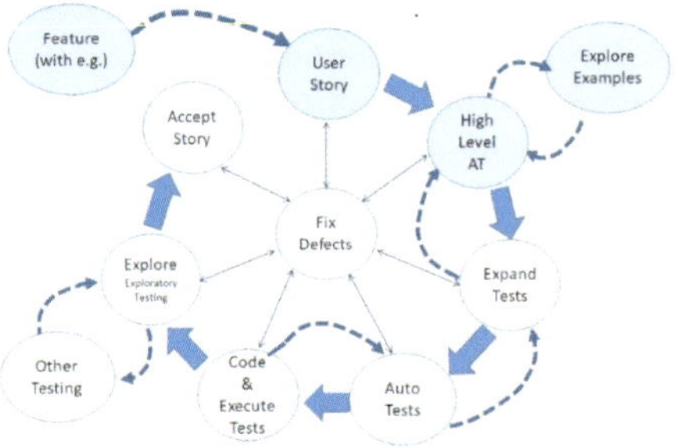

Figure 4.1: Acceptance test-driven development (ATDD)

Teams practicing Specification by Example (SBE) start by identifying goals around the story using an approach like impact mapping (See more in Chapter 5). The team then elicits key examples, which become the specifications, during a specification workshop. As development proceeds, examples are refined and turned into executable specifications to validate the product frequently. These executable examples, as with BDD and ATDD, become living documentation of the application. When Gojko Adzic coined the term Specification by Example, he deliberately did not use the word "test" to describe any of the activities.

Why examples help

Looking at each new capability from a variety of perspectives helps a team be more likely to pinpoint the value customers get from each new capability. That diversity helps each team member overcome unconscious biases and "think outside the box." When each stakeholder is asked for concrete examples of system behavior, teams look at those examples, and it's easy to see discrepancies. It is also easier to dig down to the minimum specific value of what customers need and enables teams to deliver "just enough" of the right thing.

We'll show you what we mean by using an example scenario.

Story: As a Canadian shopper, I want to give the cashier cash and I expect the correct change so that I only pay the right amount for my groceries. The cash register reports the correct amount of change to give.

Scenario: The happy path where the shopper gives more than the amount of the groceries and receives the correct change.

> **Given** I am a Canadian shopper and have purchased groceries worth $4.97,
>
> **When** I give the cashier $5.00,
>
> **Then** I expect to get $0.05 change.

Note: By using this example, a business rule that the team may not have considered is that in Canada, there are no pennies in use, so the number is rounded up or down, and change is given to the nearest nickel (0.05).

One of Janet's favorite ways to show examples is in a tabular format. It quickly shows what you are missing and what people are thinking as they have the discussion. Each line can become a test. Figure 4.2 shows this format for the scenario we used above.

Grocery total	Cash given	Change returned	Test
4.97	5.00	0.05	Happy path
4.97	4.00	0.00	Not enough cash
4.97	10.00	5.05	Happy path

Figure 4.2: Example of a tabular format of using concrete examples

There are so many good ways to structure conversations where teams can elicit examples. Jeff Patton's story mapping[4] helps the entire team walk their user's journey through their product. We like to capture specific business rules as well as examples that illustrate them with example mapping. Structured conversations using Ellen Gottesdiener and Mary Gorman's 7 product dimensions[5] ensure teams get examples of many different aspects of value. Any technique that promotes face-to-face collaboration in small cross-functional groups is worth trying. See Chapter 7 in *More Agile Testing* for more details and stories.

This is your foundation

Getting delivery and business team members together to gather examples is key to delivering value to customers at a frequent and sustainable pace. It enables teams to build the all-important shared understanding before they start coding. It helps everyone

[4]https://www.jpattonassociates.com/user-story-mapping/

[5]https://discovertodeliver.com/image/data/Resources/visuals/DtoD-7-Product-Dimensions.pdf

stay grounded in reality. The concrete examples become executable tests that ensure we build the right thing and that thing keeps working correctly into the future until customers want to change it.

> ***Hint:*** *When you find yourself in a hand-wavy discussion about requirements for a feature or an argument over how a certain capability should behave, STOP. Ask for an example. Even better, get the group to start drawing examples on the whiteboard (real or virtual). You'll save lots of time and get closer to building the right thing.*

Chapter 5: Enabling Collaboration

Collaboration within a team and between teams is one of the cornerstones that make agile teams successful. However, we find that many teams have no idea how to get started with building those relationships. In this chapter, we will talk about a few very simple practices that can help you and your team get traction.

Collaborate with customers

Let's start with collaborating with the customer – usually represented by a product owner. If teams don't understand what problem the customer is trying to solve, they may solve the wrong one. It is essential that teams work with their customer to understand their true needs.

First, we strongly suggest that everyone on the team understands the domain. This can be accomplished by working closely with end users, asking for examples or scenarios, or even drawing pictures on whiteboards to understand differences and clarify meanings.

Questions such as these will make the customer consider the usage and the associated risk.

> "How will you use this?"
>
> "What's the worst that can happen?"

Testers can facilitate developer-customer communication, but it's important not to get in the way. We call the practice of getting a tester, a programmer, and a business expert (product owner, product manager, or business analyst) together to talk about a user story, the "Power of Three." George Dinwiddie refers to it as the **Three Amigos**[6]. It is a powerful way to build shared understanding about stories, features, and how they fit into the product.

> ***Hint:*** *Gather the tester, programmer, and business expert, and perhaps one or two other roles, together anytime a question comes up. For example, a developer pair is working on a new story, and one of the business-facing tests fails. They go talk to a tester and say they think the test is expecting the wrong behavior. That's the time to grab a product owner and have a three-way discussion. This quick conversation saves so much time later trying to fix a defect that made it into the code.*

Depending on the product and the type of features being developed, more perspectives may be needed, such as from a UX designer, a data expert, or an operations expert.

Figure 5.1: Invite the right people

Impact mapping

Frameworks such as **impact mapping**[7] are helpful in deciding what features we should build and maybe even determine what the priority should be. Start with the goal of a feature (the "why"). Then

[6]https://www.agileconnection.com/article/three-amigos-strategy-developing-user-stories
[7]https://www.impactmapping.org/

identify who might help us achieve that goal and who might get in our way. For each "who," ask how they might help or hinder us in achieving the goal (those are the impacts). Lastly, think about what deliverables might result from each impact (the "what"). This exercise helps the team understand the big picture and the reasons behind what they are developing.

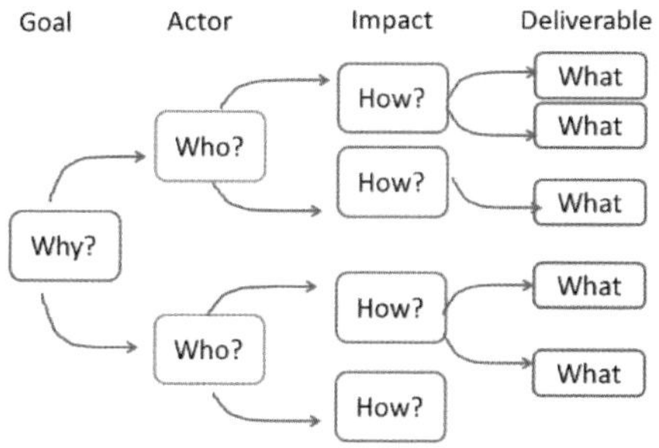

Figure 5.2: Impact mapping

It answers the question "How will we know if this feature achieves the goal after we release it?"

Ask questions

It's common that a feature planning meeting starts with a discussion about how to implement the feature. Sometimes the product owner has come with her own ideas: "Take the same code as we use for discount codes and make them negative amounts so we can add surcharges." (Yes, Lisa had that exact experience.) It is important not to let that happen – start with the why.

When you get together with a business stakeholder such as a product owner to talk about upcoming features, the first question to ask is, "Why are we doing this feature?" Other good questions: "What problem will this solve for the business, the customer, or the end user?"

QA stands for "Question Asker" – an idea we got from Pete Walen. Testers routinely ask questions that nobody else thinks of asking, so if you don't have a tester on the team, try designating a question-asker role.

Experienced teams often build quality criteria into the way they do work. For example, if they want to prevent security issues such as cross-site scripting (XSS) and SQL injection, it is probably built into the architecture of the system.

However, in our experience, business stakeholders often assume incorrectly that the technical team already knows what quality attributes are important – attributes like how many concurrent users will be using the product, what devices need to be supported, or how fast the perceived response time of an application needs to be. See Chapter 7 for more on quality attributes.

Asking specific as well as open-ended questions help expose hidden assumptions.

- "Is it possible we could implement this feature and not solve the problem?"
- "What will users do before using this feature?"
- "What will they do afterwards?"

Example mapping

Matt Wynne introduced us to the idea of example mapping[8], and we found it to be a great way to explore a new feature and the value it should deliver. Work with the product owner or other stakeholders about the business rules in a "Power of Three" type discussion. Business rules are great places to start exploring a feature, since they can help us slice a feature into stories as well as get a shared understanding of how the feature should behave.

---

[8]https://cucumber.io/blog/example-mapping-introduction/

Matt Wynne's example-mapping technique is a highly effective basis for this type of conversation because concrete examples are used to help clarify our understanding of the rules. As the conversation continues, keep the main goal in mind, and focus on the value the feature delivers to customers and end users. Teams often find that more business rules are exposed as a result of using real examples.

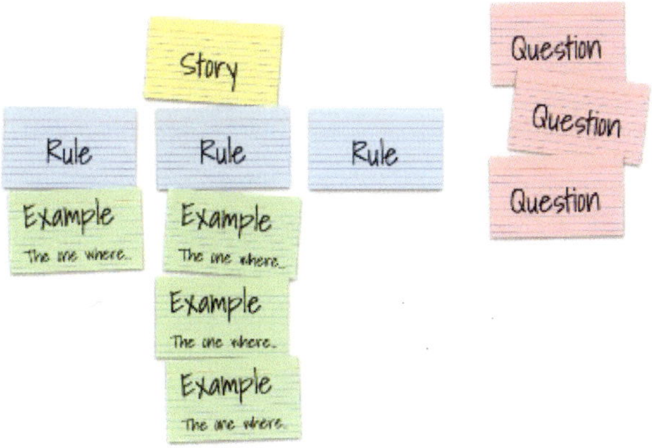

Figure 5.3: Example mapping

Using example mapping to elicit business rules, examples, and questions that need answering is an effective way to make sure the larger team starts on the same page when they plan the iteration.

Build trust using visibility

Testing allows teams to identify risks so customers can make the best decisions, which in turn builds trust. When the team asks for their input, customers gain confidence that they will get working software.

We can use mind maps, flow diagrams, context diagrams, state diagrams, or other tools to look at dependencies and ripple effects of each new feature. If our features aren't easily understood and used by everyone, they can't provide the intended value. Keeping an eye on the big picture is one strength that testers bring to agile teams.

Drawing on a whiteboard while discussing a story is a proven way to optimize communication. Getting up and moving helps people think and learn.

> ***Hint:*** *Grab a marker and some cards, stickies, a white-board. Get people to stand up and actively participate by drawing or moving index cards or sticky notes around.*

Figure 5.4: Use visibility to create trust

If there are remote participants, use online collaborative tools to help. Our teams have found that using mind maps, either on a physical whiteboard or via a real-time collaborative tool such as Mindmup, can be extremely effective in helping to identify the unknowns and find creative solutions.

These types of visual aids enable teams to ask better and more focused questions. Anytime the team encounters a problem, they find a way to make it visible, so that they can start thinking of experiments to make the problem smaller.

Chapter 6: Explore Continuously

More agile teams are finding value in exploratory testing, but it's still a new or unknown idea to many teams. We'll start by explaining the purpose of exploratory testing and what's involved.

In *Explore It!*, Elisabeth Hendrickson defines exploratory testing as "...**simultaneously** designing and executing tests to learn about the **system**, using your insights from the last **experiment** to inform the next."

In exploratory testing, a person interacts with the system and observes actual behavior, designing small experiments. Based on what they learn, they adapt the experiment and continue to learn more about the system. In the process, they may make surprising discoveries, including implications of interactions that no one had considered. Exploratory testing exposes misunderstandings about what the software is supposed to do.

Testers, programmers, or other team members who perform exploratory testing need to be open to observe, learn, use critical thinking skills, and challenge expectations. The goal of exploratory testing is to reduce risk and gain confidence in the product. There are no scripts or lists of expected outputs. Instead, a goal is identified, with resources (or variations), and a mission. Team members take notes as they explore and learn and debrief with other team members and business stakeholders later. As a result of an exploratory testing session, the tester may show any bugs found to teammates or propose new features or stories that may be needed.

Exploratory testing is a disciplined approach to testing. It is not to be confused with ad hoc testing, which is done without any planning or documentation, or monkey testing, which entails entering random inputs and random actions to see what breaks. Think about the difference between wandering randomly (perhaps lost) and exploring thoughtfully (to gain insight and with a purpose). We'll introduce a few techniques that might help you explore with purpose.

Personas, jobs, and roles

Testing a new product with a fresh set of eyes is a gift! There are not as many preconceptions about how the product should behave, and people's confirmation bias is not as strong. A new pair of eyes are better able to observe the product objectively, although of course everyone has unconscious cognitive biases. Lisa has noticed that when she pairs with new testers on her team, they immediately notice bugs that have been there all along, but nobody else could "see" them!

Assuming a persona[9], or a role, enables a team member to test a product they know inside and out with a fresh perspective; unconscious cognitive biases such as inattentional blindness[10] and confirmation bias[11] can be overcome.

A persona is a fictitious user the team creates with characteristics such as age, educational background, experience, personality quirks, profession, and so on. Some teams have a defined set of personas representing their target customer base that they use as they design new features. Figure 6.1 shows a hacker type of persona that you could use for testing.

---

[9]https://www.stickyminds.com/article/how-pragmatic-personas-help-you-understand-your-end-user

[10]http://www.theinvisiblegorilla.com/gorilla_experiment.html

[11]https://en.wikipedia.org/wiki/Confirmation_bias

Figure 6.1: Hacker persona

Combining personas with jobs or roles is even better for exploratory testing. Here's an example.

> *Jill, an executive assistant, is 30 years old, always in a hurry with too much to do, and looks for shortcuts as she uses the product. Test your team's hotel reservation application as Jill, who is booking a hotel at the last minute for her boss.*

When a tester assumes Jill's persona, she's likely to use the feature's capabilities in a different way than she normally would. For example, she might discover that clicking on the submit button multiple times out of impatience causes duplicate reservations.

Workflows and tours

A common way to explore is to go through expected workflows or user journeys in the application. Start with one journey and then explore variations on it. In that hotel-booking application, an obvious journey is searching for a specific location and date range for a certain number of guests, choosing a room, and entering address information to confirm. A variation on that approach would be to try to enter an address from a different country. Does the form accept multiple formats for postal code? Does it do validation on the postal code versus the street address?

Another popular approach is to use tours. Compare it to taking a tour in a travel destination. As a tourist, if you go to Paris, you might like to see several landmarks: the Eiffel Tower, the Louvre, Arc de Triomphe, or maybe even Notre Dame cathedral. Once you've done that, repeat the tour but go to the sights in a different order. Things may look different! The same thing happens in software. Trying the landmark tour[12] uses different features and capabilities in different orders and may cause unexpected behavior.

> ***Hint***: *Search for "exploratory test tours" on the internet and you'll find many different ideas – we suggest designing your own.*

Figure 6.2: Landmark tour

Risks and value to the customer

Teams often overlook business risks or what is of value to a customer. Exploratory test sessions can be designed to focus on these aspects to uncover hidden assumptions. Asking the question, "What is the worst thing that can happen?" may expose a risk that needs exploring. For example, if theft of customer data is a huge risk, then the team wants to spend extra time exploring the security aspects of the product.

The flip side of risk is value, so ask, "What is the best thing that can happen?" and explore around that business value.

[12]https://blogs.msdn.microsoft.com/james_whittaker/2009/04/06/tour-of-the-month-the-landmark-tour/

Explore in pairs or groups

Exploring can happen at any time. Programmers may explore during coding to shorten their feedback loop for visual issues, or testers may explore for browser compatibility. However, we recommend pairing with someone to get the most out of the experience (Figure 6.2).

Figure 6.3: Pairing

One way to explore at the feature level is with groups. One of Lisa's teams often got people together for ad hoc or exploratory test sessions for extra confidence on major or risky features. Collaborating to test concurrency issues is a great example of this. More eyes on the problem means better chances of something being found.

Much like mob programming, mob testing[13] can be used for exploratory testing. This means there is one driver (a role that rotates every few minutes) with multiple people helping by asking questions or making suggestions. Multiple perspectives may uncover impacts to other parts of the system.

Charters

In her book *Explore It!* Elisabeth Hendrickson details how to use charters for effective exploratory testing. Charters help you organize the information you need to learn about your application

[13] https://www.stickyminds.com/article/amplified-learning-mob-testing

into appropriately focused time-boxed sessions. These work well in combination with personas, jobs, and roles.

Elisabeth's template looks like this:

> **Explore** <target>
>
> **With** <resources>
>
> **To discover** <information of value to someone>

Considering the resources (or types of variations, as Janet likes to think of them) that are going to be used is a good way to start writing a charter. For example, security testing may need to test various format exploits. A charter can be written to explore several pages in the UI with these exploits. The following example shows one possibility.

> **Explore** the user signup page for 30 minutes
>
> **With** cross-site scripting exploits
>
> **To discover** any vulnerabilities

We like to time-box our sessions to help with focusing the charter. One simple way to do this is to add the time limit to the charter itself, as in our previous example.

Lisa likes to introduce people to exploratory testing by having them get into small groups to test toys and games for young children. They first create a persona, such as: "Judy is a very strong, active four-year-old." Then they test a game designed for ages 3–6 with a charter:

> **Explore** the game as Judy
>
> **Using** all her energy, unexpected movements, and strength
>
> **To discover** whether the game is safe for her age group

If they're able to break off a small piece that's a choking hazard, the game may not be safe. That's a different way to test than if you simply used the game as your adult self.

There are other ways to write charters. Some teams use mind maps, while others use mnemonics or simply write a sentence about what they want to explore.

Executing, learning, steering

People often get stuck trying to write or execute their first charter.

> ***Hint:*** *We suggest that if you find yourself in this position (stuck), don't think too hard the first time. Write it, then try it. Use your observation skills, your critical thinking, and your intuition.*

As charters are executed, the explorer learns and can write new charters. We also encourage notetaking. One advantage to pairing is that the person not driving can write the notes. We also believe that debriefing with other team members after the exploration is key to learning and sharing information.

Additional techniques

Other techniques help us "think outside the box." For example, Mike Talks has his "Oblique Testing" cards[14] that can help the tester down a path that might not have been considered otherwise. Beren van Daele's TestSphere[15] cards also get testers thinking and talking about their testing in different ways. As human beings, our unconscious biases can keep us from seeing important problems. Using cards like this can offset those biases and help teams be more creative.

[14]https://leanpub.com/obliquetesting

[15]https://www.ministryoftesting.com/dojo/series/testsphere

Leverage tools for effective exploring

Exploratory testing is human-centric, but automated scripts or tools can be used to generate test data or to set the scene. Other tools can assist exploring as well. For example, emulators can be used for embedded or mobile devices, although real devices do need to be tested and explored as well. Resources like log files can be used to spot "silent" failures or potential data loss. For example, one of Janet's teams started highlighting warnings to make them more visible, which exposed a major issue in how one method was used incorrectly. Tools like recorders can keep track of what pages have been visited or what data was used, so it can be replayed if something unexpected was found.

Chapter 7: Testing Quality Attributes

Quality attributes – or as some people like to call them, non-functional requirements – are often overlooked when discussing a new feature or story. A quality attribute defines the properties under which a feature must operate. Rather than thinking about them as an "add-on," we prefer to think of them as a constraint the team must consider with every feature or story.

Defining quality attributes

Two main types of quality attributes that need to be considered are development and operational attributes. Development attributes include code maintainability, code reuse, and testability – the "how" we develop our code. That's internal or technology-facing quality and is owned by the software delivery team.

When people talk about quality attributes, they usually mean the operational attributes. Ellen Gottesdiener and Mary Gorman classify some of the quality attributes in Figure 7.1 as operational or development attributes.

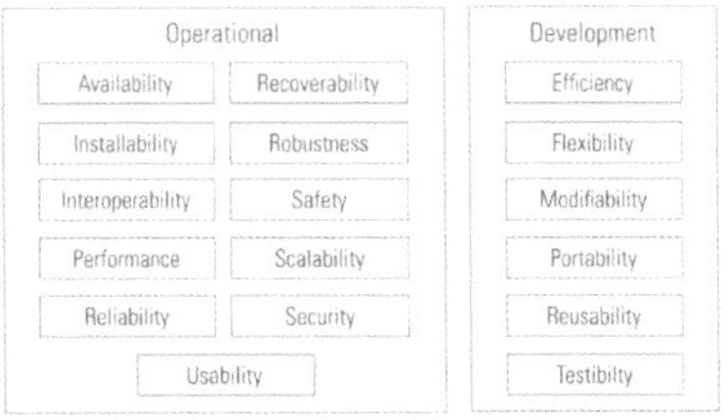

Figure 7.1: Quality attributes meta model

Many of these quality attributes are technology-facing (see Chapter 9: Agile Testing Quadrants for an explanation). If the business stakeholders don't understand them well, the delivery team can help them set the appropriate quality levels for each attribute.

Mitigating risks by collaborating early

Every product or organization has unique needs and risks that need to be assessed. By considering what quality attributes are important to your customers, the team can talk about the risks for the product. For example, Janet worked on a team where reliability was the most important quality attribute (although not the only one). The team asked themselves, "What do we need to be able to prove reliability?" When answering the question, the organization realized they needed to invest in a complete reliability testing environment where the build could be deployed at the end of every iteration to run a complete set of automated tests along with some exploratory tests. The team worked to get the automated tests and simulations working with every story.

Some teams think about their quality attributes after they deliver the functionality, and they create stories for the "non-functional" requirements. This is generally not a good idea because it may mean having to go back and re-do the architecture or code design.

These attributes may in fact be higher priority than functional or behavioral requirements. Valuable functionality in some areas doesn't overcome lack of security or performance in some business domains. Teams that wait too late in the cycle to test these attributes (often during the endgame just before release) hit a total roadblock. These types of issues are usually design issues and can't be fixed that late in the release cycle.

As a delivery team, be proactive. Don't wait for the product owner to start the conversation. She's probably thinking about feature capabilities and taking quality attributes for granted. As a team, consider which aspects of quality are most valuable to customers and the business. A good way to start is by drawing a context diagram of the proposed new feature to see how it interacts with other capabilities or systems. Knowing the dependencies and potentially fragile areas early means there is enough time to make the right design decisions and ensure the team has the necessary technical knowledge. The team might plan to do a spike (an experiment or investigation story) to explore potential designs and architecture.

Release or feature planning offer great opportunities to ask business stakeholders questions like these:

- What's the worst thing that can happen after we release this capability? Does that make it high risk?
- Is it ok if the system or a system capability is down for some amount of time? If not, what is the maximum time or percentage of time it can be down?
- For a web-based app, what browsers might customers use?
- Can we assume that customers will be using mobile devices? Would that include phones and tablets, and does that mean both Apple and android? What about ......?
- How will we know if the feature is successful once we release it?

Planning for pre-release testing

Some quality attributes might require more testing immediately before the release when all components of the feature set are connected. For example, the team may do load or performance testing in a staging environment to get a final baseline. If the team uses blue/green deploys[16] in a cloud infrastructure, they may do this testing on the idle production environment.

Teams can use release feature toggles and other techniques to hide new features from customers until they test various quality attributes in production. Once they are confident in the level of quality for all aspects of the feature, they can toggle the feature on. (See more on testing in production in Chapter 8: Testing in DevOps.)

Planning for later learning

Asking that last question – How will we know if the feature is successful once we release it? – is a great way for the team to talk about the purpose of the new feature and how they can measure whether it meets the desired goals. Provisioning data for analytics tools needs to be planned into the stories for each feature. At the story level, think about how the team can monitor the system to measure usage and quality of the attribute. The team may need new tools for appropriate logging and monitoring.

At the task level, the programmers should be thinking about instrumenting the code so that the team can measure with automated tests or monitoring tools (see Figure 7.2). The solution might be as simple as running an optimizer on a new database query or using a static analysis tool to check that the code meets accessibility standards. A more holistic approach, such as instrumenting every event

[16] https://docs.cloudfoundry.org/devguide/deploy-apps/blue-green.html

in the code so that production issues can be quickly pinpointed and fixed, may be appropriate.

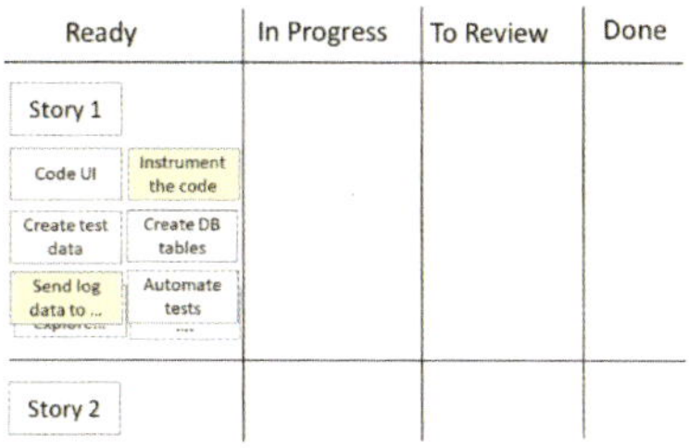

Figure 7.2: Task board with future in mind

Regulatory compliance

Regulatory compliance isn't always deemed a quality attribute, but like the quality attributes we've mentioned, you need to consider it from the beginning. Compliance does not necessarily mean stacks of documents, but there is usually extra work involved for the team, and it's wise to plan early.

Organizations need to work together with auditors and regulatory agencies to understand what information is required to show compliance. It is important that everyone has the same vision of an appropriately disciplined approach. For example, if the team has automated tests that run every day and the tests provide living documentation in the form of test results, can those be used as evidence to support the approach or coverage? Both of us have worked with teams that needed to show compliance (medical devices and financial) and did it with very little "extra" work. See Chapter 21, "Agile Testing in Regulated Environments" in *More Agile Testing* for more examples and information.

Chapter 8: Testing in DevOps

Software development has always included the process of getting new changes to the software into production for customers to use. In the past, much of this process was manual. There are new tools and practices for creating software artifacts and deploying them into test and production environments. But the basic process is the same. Teams have many testing activities to help them feel confident about the changes they make to their production product. There are new terms for some of this testing, but basic testing skills are still relevant.

The DevOps movement grew out of the idea that some organizations had embraced agile development but left their entire operations staff out of the transition. It's also a result of the move to cloud-hosted applications and infrastructure as code replaced command line interfaces. Roles have adapted. Operations specialists learn how to code. Programmers take responsibility for their code even after it is in production, instead of throwing it over the wall to operations.

Testers also adapt their own skills and activities. They contribute in many ways, such as helping to design the automated test suites that provide reliable and valuable information, optimizing the delivery pipeline, and testing infrastructure code to ensure reliable execution.

Chapter 23 in *More Agile Testing* goes into detail about how operations specialists can help the delivery team improve quality by setting up test environments, helping to implement test automation frameworks, generating test data, and more.

Continuous delivery and deployment

Teams practicing continuous delivery (CD) have a deployable release candidate each time a new change is committed to the code repository and subsequently passes successfully through a deployment pipeline. The pipeline starts with continuous integration, which may include automated test suites at different levels such as unit, API, and full workflow through the user interface. It may include other steps such as static code analysis for automated deployments to various environments. The business stakeholders can decide to deploy the release candidate to production and may do so many times per day. Figure 8.1 shows an example of a continuous delivery pipeline.

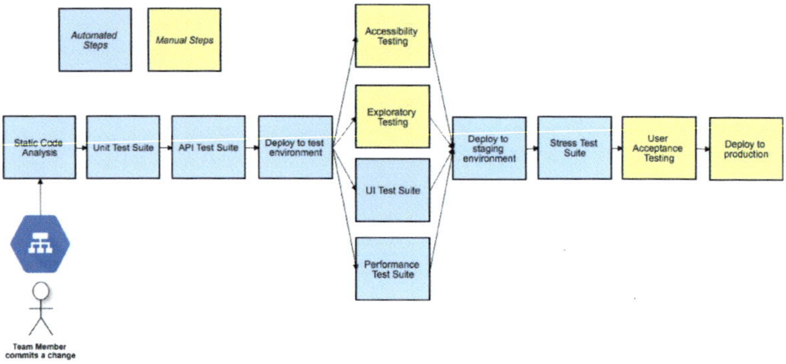

Figure 8.1: Continuous delivery pipeline

Continuous deployment (also CD) is the same process, except that each successful release candidate automatically deploys to production. Figure 8.2 shows an example of a continuous deployment pipeline.

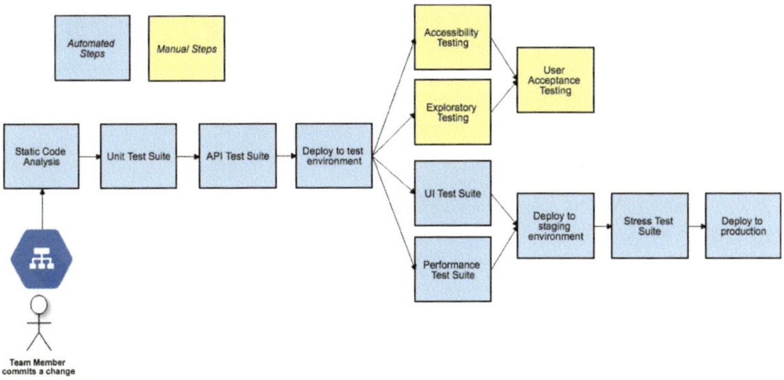

Figure 8.2: Continuous deployment pipeline

This sounds as scary as testing in production if you haven't done it before. If you release multiple times per day, how can you possibly fit in all the testing that you need to do? Human-centric testing, whether tests the team hasn't automated yet or testing activities like exploratory and accessibility testing, is as much a part of a delivery pipeline as automated tests.

The key is recognizing **the difference between deploying and releasing**.

Thanks to techniques such as release feature toggles, it's possible to hide changes from customers until all necessary testing is completed. Testing can be done asynchronously.

Continuous delivery or deployment represents a high standard of achievement for a team. Delivery team members and business stakeholders need to create a shared understanding of each feature and story to be delivered. The developers master ways of hiding features from some (or all) customers until they are ready to release that feature. The delivery pipeline must be fast in order to potentially deploy daily or multiple times per day. That requires a good infrastructure, which means more code to build and test. There are many new skills to master. When each team member brings their T-shaped skills[17] and everyone collaborates, the team can more easily solve problems and continue to shorten their feedback loops represented in the pipeline.

Testing in production

At one time, the term "testing in production" sounded like "Throw the code into production and let the customers find the bugs and tell us," or "Let's test in production and hope that we don't affect anybody's account." Sadly, some teams did just that. Today, the words "testing in production" have a less fearful connotation. Testing in production has become a necessity in many cases, but it does not mean releasing poor quality code and letting customers find the bugs!

Testing in production helps companies in multiple ways. It's usually impossible to create a test environment that looks exactly like production. There is no easy way to really know what the software will do until it's in the production environment.

Techniques such as release feature toggling enable teams to "turn on" specific functionality to specific customers to get quick feedback. Sometimes this is called a learning release or minimal viable product (MVP). A/B testing may be the most well-known testing-in-production technique, showing different designs to different people and judging which lead to the most "click-throughs" or sales.

Sophisticated analytics and tracing can show details such as how an individual user navigates through the application, or aggregate statistics like what percentage of customers are using a specific capability. Removing unused features can be just as important as adding popular new ones, since every line of code has a maintenance cost and adds risk. Testing in production is about monitoring and observing.

[17] https://lisacrispin.com/tag/t-shaped-skills/

Monitoring and observability

The importance of monitoring system health in production has existed as long as software systems have logged pertinent information about events in the system. Teams can set up alerts for certain types of errors or for exceeding an error budget – for example, "Post an alert when the number of 503 errors goes up by 10% over average." When alerted, team members dig into the log files and analytics to investigate the problem so they can resolve it.

Professional testers know that it's not possible to predict all the possible errors that can occur in production! In recent years, this has given rise to a new practice called observability, often referred to as "o11y," representing the 11 characters between the 'o' and the 'y' in the English alphabet. Teams that practice o11y instrument and log every single event in their production code so it can be analyzed by appropriate tools when needed. Using tools and experiments, teams study information from structured log data, metrics, and traces to learn different things about their product than what can be learned in a test environment. This is an area where testers, with their ability to notice unusual patterns and identify risks, contribute value. As Abby Bangser[18] has said, it is a form of tool-assisted exploratory testing.

Observability lets teams respond quickly when a user reports a problem that the team has never seen before, or when system metrics show unusual patterns indicating a potential problem. The structured log data enables the team to trace user activity and quickly identify where the system started behaving incorrectly. This allows teams to revert a change or deploy a fix, often in a matter of minutes. This ability to recover so quickly from production failures lets the team release these continual small changes to the product fearlessly, and it's what makes continuous delivery or deployment a safe practice.

---

[18]https://club.ministryoftesting.com/t/power-hour-curious-stuck-or-need-guidance-on-devops-or-observability/24963/3

New technology brings us new capabilities

In the past few years, "big data" storage has become affordable even for small companies. Teams can log information about every event that occurs in any test or production environment. Powerful technology, including artificial intelligence (AI) and machine learning (ML), has sped up processing and analysis of these huge amounts of data. We can quickly learn how customers are using our products, discover problems before they do, and quickly recover from failures.

Testing in production is just one part of any team's approach to building quality into their product. They still plan and execute all the appropriate testing activities along with writing the production code. They can also observe production use and run risk-free tests in production to add another level of confidence and reliability. Figure 8.3 is a wonderful graphic by Cindy Sridharan from her article *Monitoring and Observability*[19], and represents how teams test trying to simulate production, monitor for predictable failures in production, and use observability to catch anything that slips through those other quality-driven efforts.

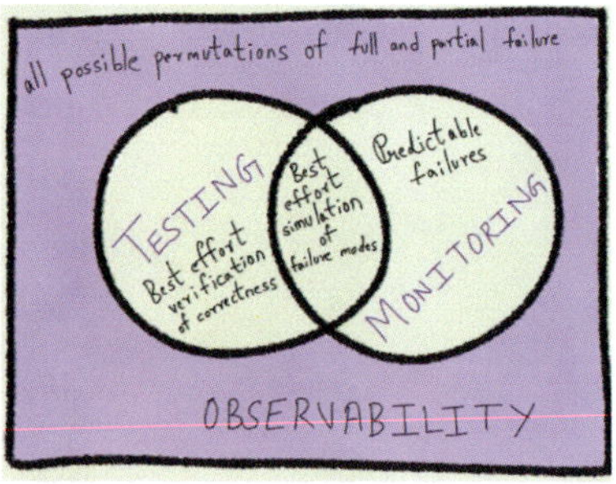

Figure 8.3: Cindy Sridharan's testing, monitoring, and observability

---

[19]https://medium.com/@copyconstruct/testing-in-production-the-safe-way-18ca102d0ef1

SECTION 3: Helpful Models

We have found visual models an essential ingredient in helping teams plan and execute all necessary testing activities and formulate an effective test automation strategy. In this section, we explain how to use the Agile Testing Quadrants to identify all the types of tests that are needed for each new feature set or story, and make sure they are done when they are the most effective. Then we look at how to use visual models such as the Test Automation Pyramid to guide team conversations about a realistic automation strategy that works for their context.

- Chapter 9: The Agile Testing Quadrants
- Chapter 10: Visualizing a Test Automation Strategy

Chapter 9: The Agile Testing Quadrants

Brian Marick first wrote about the agile testing quadrants (Figure 9.1) in 2003, when Lisa and Janet were trying to figure out how to talk about testing to the agile community, especially the testers. At that time, most of the agile folks were discussing only "customer tests" and "programmer tests." A lot of teams were focused only on functional acceptance tests – how the features should behave. Today, this is still a potential pitfall for teams transitioning to agile. The quadrants gave us a way to discuss all the different types of testing that a team might need to consider. They help us see the big picture.

The agile testing quadrants are a taxonomy of different types of testing. We use it as a thinking tool to help teams discuss what testing activities they might need and make sure they have the right people, resources, and environments to perform them.

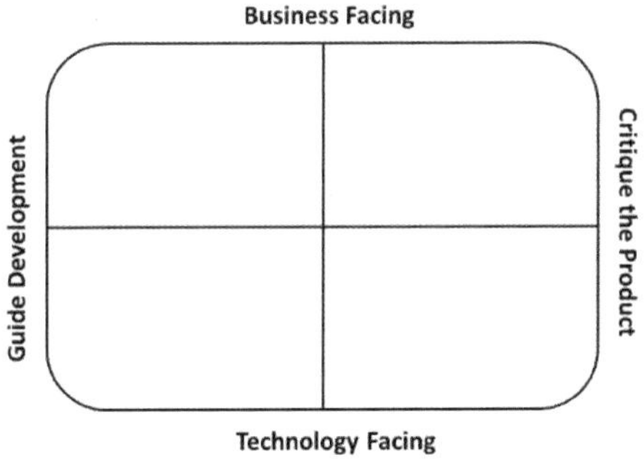

Figure 9.1: Agile Testing Quadrants

Tests on the left-hand side are those that guide development, the ones that are written before coding happens or concurrently as coding proceeds. The tests on the right-hand side are those that critique (evaluate) the product after coding is complete. Tests on the left help prevent defects. Tests on the right find defects in the code or perhaps identify missing features.

The top half of the quadrants focuses on tests that are readable by business stakeholders. These tests answer the question, "Are we building the right thing?" The bottom half includes tests that are written by and for technical team members. The business stakeholders probably care about the end results, but they would not try to read the tests. The top half is about external quality as defined by the business. The bottom half is about internal code or infrastructure correctness.

The quadrants are numbered for ease of reference. The four quadrants are labeled as:

- **Quadrant 1** (Q1): Technology-facing tests that guide development
- **Quadrant 2** (Q2): Business-facing tests that guide development
- **Quadrant 3** (Q3): Business-facing tests that critique the product
- **Quadrant 4** (Q4): Technology-facing tests that critique the product

The agile testing quadrants model helps teams think through testing activities that are needed to give confidence to the product they are building. It also helps to build a common testing language with the team and with the organization if used to help communicate across teams. Janet's favorite thing about this model is that it not only represents a holistic view into testing but also makes the whole team's responsibility for testing activities visible.

Each team has its own distinct combination of business domain, product, skills, product maturity, technical stack, regulatory oversight, and more. The model can be applied to represent the testing required in each context. In Figure 9.2, we share some typical types of tests that might be found in each quadrant.

> ***Hint**: Remember: Use these examples as a guideline. It's a tool, not a rule, and there are lots of gray areas. Your team's context is unique, and your quadrants should be too. Apply the model to the testing you need to do.*

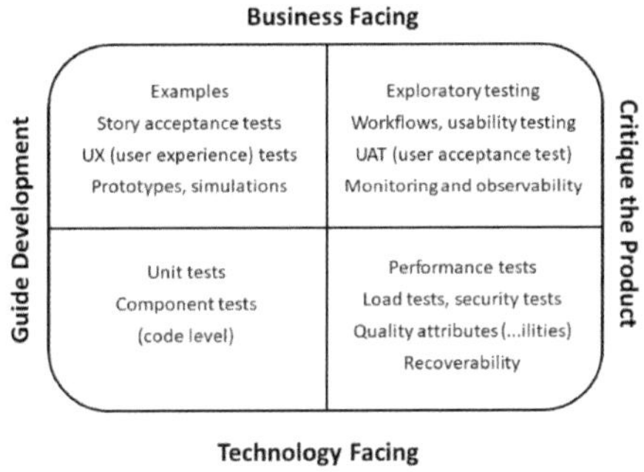

Figure 9.2: Examples of testing types for the quadrants

What tests in what order?

We have numbered the quadrants 1, 2, 3, 4 simply for ease of reference. It's a mouthful to say "Business-facing tests that guide development," so we say, "Quadrant 2" or "Q2." The numbers are not intended to represent that the types of testing activities should be done in that order. As the team plans their testing, they will think about the appropriate time to do each testing activity.

Here's an example. A team decides to start using a new architecture for the new features going forward. They need to be sure that the architecture will scale appropriately to accommodate a certain number of users and a potential load on the system. The team does a "spike," which means they write some throw-away code solely for the purpose of testing out the architecture. They do load and performance testing on the "spike" to see if it meets response time requirements and remains stable. If they're satisfied, they delete the spike and start working on stories for a new feature, this time following their usual development practices. If they're not satisfied, they may re-think the architecture and repeat the process.

For feature development, most teams probably start in Q2. They might draw prototypes on paper and show them to potential customers. The delivery and business team might have a story-mapping or specification workshop to discuss features and slice them into stories. During backlog refinement or story-readiness workshops, the team can use activities such as example mapping to extract more details.

Once the team starts developing a story, they work on tests from Q1, writing unit tests as part of test-driven development. They may simultaneously be working on story tests in Q2. If enough of a feature is delivered to explore, they may move into Q3 testing. However, if security is the number one concern for the business and customers, security testing in Q4 may be prioritized over functional story testing from Q2. Each team finds their own way of working, and it may change for different types of features or projects.

Using the quadrants

Janet and Lisa have seen teams use the quadrants in many ways. Some teams put a poster on the wall with the blank quadrants. As they plan a new feature or release, they talk about all the testing they'll need and write each type in the appropriate quadrant. They use it as a reminder about what they need to do or what they may have forgotten.

Quadrant 1

Teams can also use the quadrants to talk about what tests should be automated. Q1 tests are typically automated by the developers writing the production code. Many teams practice test-driven development (TDD), writing a small unit test for some small piece of functionality, then the code to make that test pass. Q1 tests are designed to run quickly since they test such a small area of code and generally don't include interaction with other layers of the application or databases. They give teams the fast feedback needed to make changes to the code quickly and fearlessly.

Quadrant 2

The business-facing tests that guide development in Q2 are an important foundation for most teams. Product owners, developers, testers, and others meet frequently to plan features and stories. They may use techniques such as example mapping to elicit business rules for each story along with the examples that illustrate them. Teams practicing behavior-driven development (BDD), acceptance test-driven development (ATDD), or specification by example (SBE) turn these into scenarios that specify behavior as executable tests. These scenarios can be automated as the code is written.

Quadrant 3

Tests in Q3 tend to be human-centric, learning whether the delivered stories and features provide the intended value to customers. Automation may be used to facilitate this testing via data or state setup. It's becoming more common for teams to do exploratory testing in production, using release feature toggles to "hide" new features from customers until testing is complete. Q3 tests include forms of testing in production such as monitoring analytics to learn what really happens and how customers use the features. Information learned from Q3 testing feeds back into Q2, often resulting in creating new stories or features.

Quadrant 4

Many Q4 tests depend on automation and tools, but some may require additional testing. For example, the automated tools for accessibility (often shortened to "a11y," representing the starting and ending letters and the number of letters in between) testing are still not as effective as manual exploratory testing for those capabilities. Results of these tests often feed back into Q1 activities as the team changes the code design to improve various quality attributes. Monitoring performance and errors in production, or testing for recoverability, can also be considered a type of testing that falls into Q4. Today's technology has made it feasible and safe to test in production. This doesn't mean that we let customers find bugs for us but that we learn for sure how the code behaves in a true production environment. (Details on testing in production can be found in Chapter 8.)

Defining "Done"

Use the quadrants to define what "Done" means to your team. Many teams struggle when trying to decide what testing should be included in that definition. In Chapter 3, we talked about levels of detail, and those levels apply here. Instead of defining "Done," we encourage teams to be more specific and call it "**Story Done**." Testing that can be included in "Story Done" would likely be all of Q1, all of Q2, and perhaps some of Q3 like exploratory testing.

Go one step further and define "**Feature Done**," which would include all testing for stories, but perhaps also includes tests like user acceptance testing (UAT) and exploratory testing at the feature level. We recommend that all quality attributes that could not be tested at the story level should be performed at the feature level.

You may even choose to define "**Release Done**." That would include every test that applies in your context, from every quadrant.

> ***Hint***: *Remember, when we talk about "done-ness" at story, feature, and release levels, we are not mandating that tests be done in a certain order. Rather, consider which tests guide development (prevent defects) and which ones are critiquing the product (finding defects in the code).*

Figure 9.3: Finding and "fixing" bugs

Find the models that fit your context

Many teams have found the agile testing quadrants useful in planning their testing activities. Others have adapted the quadrants model to better suit their needs, and there are many useful variations on the quadrants. You can find Chapter 8 from *More Agile Testing* available for download on agiletester.ca[20], and it includes several adaptations of the quadrants. Check our resources list for more.

Whatever model works best for you, be sure to keep it visible and use it to stimulate conversations about how to continually improve your testing.

[20]https://agiletester.ca

Chapter 10: Visualizing a Test Automation Strategy

Test automation is a constant challenge for software teams everywhere. Many teams still have no automated regression tests. Some teams feel they've mastered the process, but then they update their product to incorporate new technology that their existing automation tools can't handle. They often struggle to maintain a balance between value and maintenance cost.

Wherever an individual team is on its automation journey, it's helpful to take a step back and think about priorities and what improvements to focus on next. This chapter is not meant to give you an extensive introduction into automation but to show how using visual models can help teams design their automation strategy.

Using visual models

Getting the whole team involved in formulating a strategy for addressing different automation needs and executing that strategy is key to succeeding with automation. Visual models help guide these conversations.

The agile testing quadrants model covered in Chapter 9 can help teams plan their automation strategy as they discuss the different types of testing that are needed, as well as what skills, tools, and infrastructure they will need to complete it. In this chapter, we look at some additional models that can help teams find a successful automation strategy.

> ***Hint***: *Remember, these are thinking tools, to be used to start conversations about how your team wants to automate tests.*

The classic test automation pyramid

Mike Cohn's test automation pyramid has helped many teams since the early 2000s. We've adjusted it slightly since then (Figure 10.1) to make our intent clear, including the cloud bubble on top to represent that not all regression tests can be automated. Sometimes we need human-centric tests, which include exploratory tests (ET).

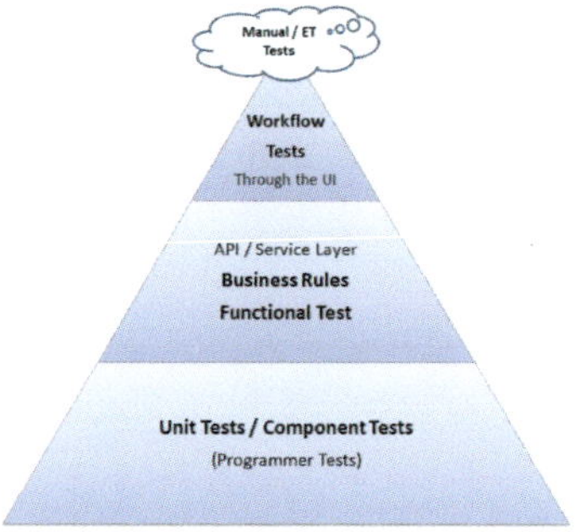

Figure 10.1: Classic Test Automation Pyramid

This model helps teams understand that in most contexts, it pays to automate tests at the most granular level of the application as possible, to provide adequate protection against regression failures. Teams that practice test-driven development (TDD) build up a solid base of unit- and component-level tests that help guide code design. These tests run very fast, so they give the team quick feedback.

With most applications, testing interactions between different layers of the architecture is required. For example, business logic usually requires interaction with the database. Doing as much automation of this type at the service or API level without going through a user interface (UI) is generally the most efficient way.

Some regressions only occur when two or more layers of the application are involved. That may require workflow tests through the UI that involve the server, database, and/or an external system. In most contexts, it's best to minimize the number of end-to-end workflow tests. These tests run slowly, are often the most brittle, and usually require the most maintenance. The cloud at the top of the pyramid includes human-centric activities such as exploratory testing and other tasks that can't be automated.

The test automation pyramid helps us think of ways to "push tests lower," maximize the regression tests that are isolated to one part of an application, and minimize those that involve multiple parts of the system. When teams plan testing for a feature, they can look at the pyramid to see where each test can most appropriately be automated.

The classic pyramid is not meant to imply that there is a certain number or percentage of automated tests at each level. Seb Rose envisions the model a bit differently, as shown in Figure 10.2.

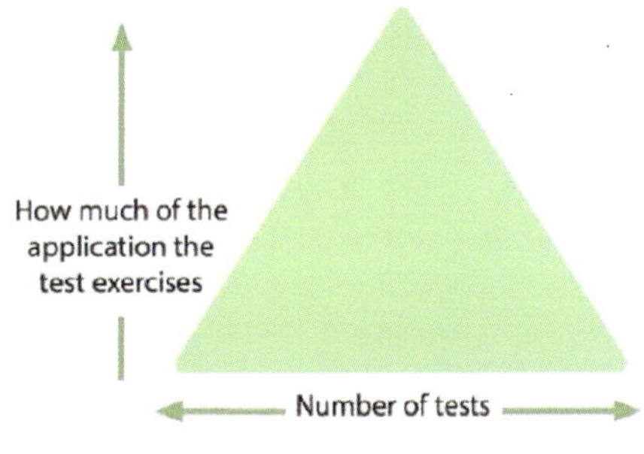

Figure 10.2: Seb Rose's version of the pyramid, number of tests vs. test coverage

Seb's model clarifies that what makes a test more expensive is the number of layers of the application it requires to execute. For example, it's possible to have a unit-level test of the UI that does not involve any other layers of the application. It's possible to use TDD for each isolated layer of the application, whether it's the server, the API, the UI, or a microservice.

There have been many adaptations of the pyramid model (and yes, the classic one is really a triangle) over the years. Chapter 15 of *More Agile Testing* includes several adaptations, including those from Alister Scott and Sharon Robson.

Teams that have automated tests can draw the "shape" of their pyramid to visualize where their current tests fit. Many teams start out with mostly UI tests and an "upside-down" pyramid or "ice cream cone[21]." Others may have an hourglass. None of these shapes are necessarily wrong, but if the current automation doesn't meet the team's needs, the visuals can help picture what changes are needed.

Conversations around a visual model help teams that are just starting their automation efforts decide their eventual goal and their first priorities.

Automated tests as living documentation

The time, cost, and effort that goes into automating different types of tests at different levels of the application are not the only considerations when putting together an automation strategy. Another consideration is remembering who needs to be able to read and understand the tests. Seb Rose's Test Automation Iceberg (Figure 10.3) reminds us that one of the most valuable attributes of automated tests is the living documentation that they provide. They're always up to date because the team keeps them passing all

[21]https://watirmelon.blog/testing-pyramids/

the time, so you can tell at any given time exactly what your system does.

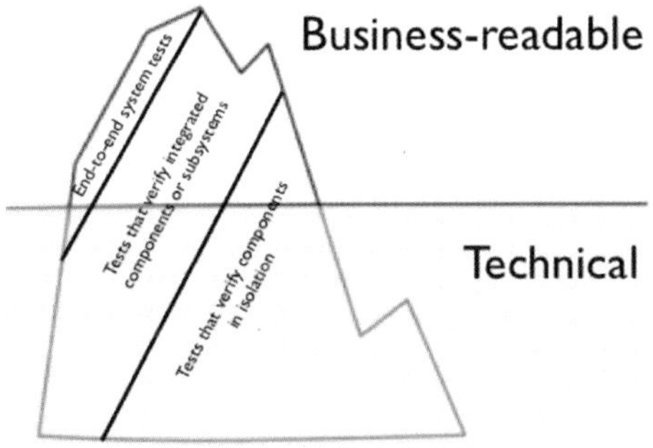

Figure 10.3: Seb Rose's test automation iceberg

Those portions of the iceberg above the waterline are tests that are business readable, while those below are not (are written in a technical language). The amount of tests will vary by team; for example, Lisa worked on a team whose product was intended for other delivery teams. Everyone on the team including the product owner could understand the automated regression tests written in low-level code. They didn't need "business-readable" tests. In other domains, it's critical that business stakeholders can understand the acceptance tests. This model helps remind us to think about what's needed in the team's context.

Extending the model

Even the most diligent automated regression test coverage may fail to identify some regression failures. No test environment is exactly like production. Some bugs may be found via "testing in production," as discussed in Chapter 8.

In her book *A Practical Guide to Testing in DevOps*, Katrina Clokie presents her DevOps bug filter. It's a helpful visual showing that unit tests can only filter out the small bugs, while different levels of integration and end-to-end tests detect progressively bigger ones. To find the fully formed bugs, teams need logging, alerting, and monitoring for their production system.

Shared responsibility

We encourage teams to share the responsibility of testing the business rules and higher levels of integration at the API level. Testers should also have visibility into the unit and component tests written by developers. As a team member, it's important to understand your team's applications and the inner workings when approaching your automation strategy.

Because automating tests through the UI tends to be more time-consuming, there's a temptation to hand that off to a separate automation team or have the testers on the team take full responsibility for it. We recommend that the developers, who are good at writing efficient, maintainable code, work together with the testers, who are good at specifying test cases, to automate tests through the UI as well as all other layers above the base level of the pyramid.

Remember, like all the other models, the test automation pyramid is a guide. Teams that get members in all roles together to ask questions, chat about the answers, draw on the whiteboard, and design experiments have the best success with automation. Visual models like the examples in this chapter help teams talk about why they're automating tests, what their biggest automation pain points are, how people with different skills could help, and what their next experiments should be. In our experience, a step-by-step approach works best.

SECTION 4: Agile Testing Today

The basics of agile testing – such as using the whole-team approach, guiding development with examples, and collaborating across roles to build quality in – are as effective today as they were 20 years ago. Is there anything we need to change to meet today's challenges? In this section, we share what some leading agile testing practitioners see changing for the role of testers. We'll wrap up with a bunch of ingredients to help teams succeed with agile testing.

- Chapter 11: A Tester's New Role
- Chapter 12: Ingredients for Success

Chapter 11: A Tester's New Role

Many teams struggle with only one tester as part of the team – or even worse, a tester who supports more than one delivery team. If the tester is the only one doing testing activities, it generally creates a bottleneck. Agile teams who deliver changes to production at every iteration (or even more frequently if they're implementing continuous delivery) cannot afford to have a single tester to do all the testing.

We can't predict the future, but it is informative to look around to see how a tester's role is changing. We asked other experienced agile testing coaches and trainers to find out what their thoughts are about the changing role of a tester. These different perspectives may help you understand how testers and teams can adapt and help build a quality culture.

Testers are quality glue for a team

Alex Schladebeck – Germany

When I started out, the tester role in a team (if the tester was even a part of the team) was often to be solely responsible for UI automation and manual testing. Over the last 12 years, I've seen a huge diversification of the role, and always in a context-dependent way based on how the team operated. I see testers working on more automation tasks, even pairing at the unit level with developers. I see them being involved at all process points. I see them organizing mob testing sessions with the team to perform exploratory testing.

I see them campaigning for better feedback loops. I've even seen testers start to fix bugs or implement features.

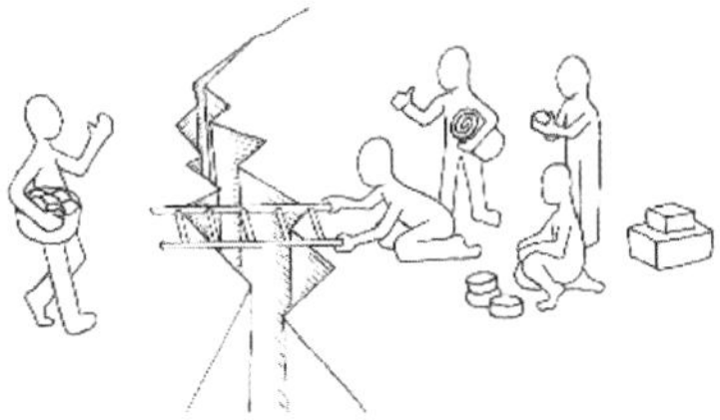

Make connections

For me, this diversification and role-blurring is a huge freedom and a great responsibility. It means that we have to ask ourselves, "How do I, my skills, and my potential to learn best fit into this team's context?" We become very much "quality and communication glue," identifying and filling in the gaps in any team.

I've started using the term "embedded quality engineer" or "embedded quality consultant" for this role. The problem with the title "tester" is that it contains the name of one of the many activities we do, so you hear questions like, "If everyone is involved in testing, why do we need a tester?" or statements like, "The developers are automating tests, so we don't need a tester role." Testing is just one of the many things that a tester does. In my opinion, we need to fight against the idea that an agile team should consist of "chimeras": a mix of different roles, or a Swiss-Army-knife team member that can do everything: requirements, UX, test, security, front and backend. Agile teams need to be diverse and cross-functional, and that means we need people with different backgrounds, interests, and specializations, without any one person being a silo or bottleneck. I think that's a balance that is achievable.

I see the tester role as consisting of multiple activities. There are things that have always been part of the role, like working with stakeholders, bringing expertise to test activities, pairing with developers and other testers, supporting the product owner, organizing and adapting the overall quality strategy, getting good test data, and identifying risk. I think there will be even more tasks that can be taken on or supported by testers in the future. Some of these might be: working with the team to ensure testability and observability for testing and monitoring in production, asking questions of the production system to explore how it is being used, honing our performance and teaching skills for exploratory testing, helping the team to focus on value (and sometimes on minimalism, i.e., the value of something not done). I also see testers starting to add "team health" to their quality attributes, looking out for the communication and stress levels of the team as a whole. These are, after all, things that can affect quality greatly.

In short, I believe that the tester role remains important. They are the person in the team whose main priority is quality. They are also the person with the passion for quality and testing, and they advocate and champion for them.

An agile tester's professional journey

Paul Carvalho – Canada

When I coach agile teams, I help the whole team learn to work together and build upon each others' strengths. A product owner brings business and industry knowledge, a programmer brings strong coding and development skills, a designer brings insights into the user's perspective and experience, and a tester brings something of value to the table as well.

A tester's professional journey starts with moving away from accidental and random testing, to thoughtful design of tests through models, techniques, and other specialized skills and knowledge. Agile puts a strong focus on working closely with others, so testers need to get out of their heads when thinking about testing and find their voice to help other team members understand the many ways to generate quality information about the systems in development. A great agile tester spends more time with a whiteboard marker in hand and pairing with other team members than anything else. It's about helping the rest of the team to see and understand more about the system, before the system is built. "Build Quality In" is more than a slogan; it is a reality that great testers can help enable on high-performing collaborative teams.

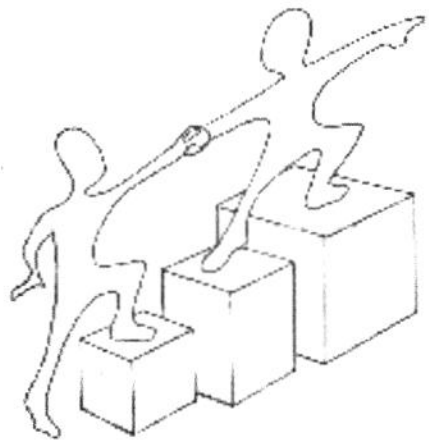

Mentor

An agile tester's professional journey progresses from random, haphazard testing, to understanding the techniques and design of good testing, to finding a voice and expressing these ideas so they may help elevate the rest of your team's performance.

As a tester, aim to enhance and grow everyone's understanding of the systems and solutions through thoughtful exploration. If you let go of the notion that you must be the one to write test cases or program automation, think about where your unique skills and insights can help carry your team.

The fascinating path of evolving as testers

Claudia Badell – Uruguay

As testers, we can contribute and add value from different perspectives: as facilitators and evangelists toward testing and quality in a product team, as coaches, as test consultants, as experts at certain types of testing (usability testing, accessibility testing, security testing, performance testing, among others), and more. Testers are no longer seen as gatekeepers for quality, so we can be seen and valued as quality advocators.

Nowadays, it is more and more frequent that testers are part of the development team and make contributions from the beginning of the development process. In my experience, the role of a tester in this context is evolving. Besides performing testing activities to support manual testing and automated checks, testers collaborate to build bridges within the team in order to reach a common understanding and engagement about testing. They also define, follow up, and adjust the testing strategies to be applied by the whole team. In addition, they share and evangelize their knowledge of testing within the team.

As technology, methodologies, and processes evolve and teams and communities mature, I believe it is important for us to have a proactive attitude to adapt to such changes. The future will bring new challenges and opportunities. Depending on the context, different skills and different testing activities may be needed, but in my experience, there are core skills that are necessary to keep pace with software development.

Experiment and find new opportunities

These skills are:

- be eager to learn and try new experiments to enhance testing strategies in the team.
- be an excellent question asker throughout the product life-cycle. Depending on the type of information that we gather, questions can be formulated in different ways. They can be made verbally or in writing, so clear and well-structured communication skills are important. They can also be made programmatically; for example, if we wanted to check certain responses between two services, technical skills are important.
- have modeling skills as a way of understanding what to test and defining testing strategies that cover the different aspects that are needed.
- have some degree of technical knowledge to collaborate in defining testability aspects of the solution while the software is being developed – for example, to support unit testing and automated integration testing.
- have a sharing and collaborative attitude.

We are in an exciting time where we can shape part of our future. How are you getting prepared for it?

Be all that you can be

Mike Talks - New Zealand

Over the last six years, my test team has gone from a single group working on one waterfall project at a time to individuals working across multiple teams.

There's a lot of talk about a whole-team approach to quality and testing, but testers as specialists are looked to lead in this space. That means creating a first-pass approach at a new story or feature, but it is also important to facilitate a discussion with the larger team about these approaches to gain feedback and explore the approach. It also means if a testing task is too onerous for testers to complete alone, they can help organise a division of labor among willing team members.

I find a frequent candidate for this is cross browser/device testing. We often test stories in the iteration using our core devices but will occasionally visit our product on a much broader range of items. This is where the team and their fresh sets of eyes can help, and a little bit of organization from the tester can make a huge difference.

Although most conversations about testing a product happen within your team, it's also useful to "catch up" with others in the same disciplines to share ideas and what's been working on other teams. This can also turn into mentoring to help individuals deal with specific problems as well as become more daring to try new ideas.

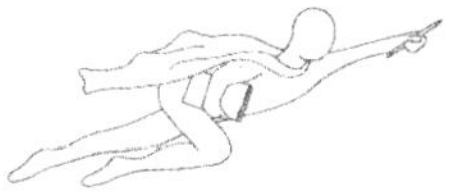

Be all you can be

Start with a conversation

Kathleen Naughton – United States

Software testing has simultaneously evolved and stood still. It has evolved to the point that some organizations have reduced the number or even eliminated testers on their teams. It has stood still because these same organizations have struggled to value the specialty skills a tester brings to teams.

In my experience, where testers have been reduced or eliminated, the teams have tried to fill in by moving closer to TDD practices so that they have a large number of automated unit tests. They try to do some intra-team testing (testing each other's code) and rely heavily on their continuous delivery pipeline to execute their automated tests. What often ends up being missed are the integration and user experience tests that are essential for high-quality products. If there are testers in these organizations, they are present to do manual testing after the code is finished. Any insights or suggestions made by these testers tend to be deprioritized in the product backlog in deferment to feature development.

Be relevant and influence those around you

I believe an essential skill that testers need to be relevant is being able to read and understand code. This allows them to understand what unit tests or other automated tests are checking and enables the identification of testing gaps that the tester can fill. It also allows for reduction in test overlap. If there are already unit or integration tests present, the testing approach can be more targeted at the end-user activities that are not covered. Another essential skill I believe is needed might be considered a soft skill. The skill of having conversations with programmers about their unit and integration tests is powerful. These conversations can lead to influencing design decisions that in turn enable higher-quality deliverables. Bringing knowledge about how to have crucial conversations enables the whole team to produce better software.

The world doesn't need more checkers

Aldo Rall - New Zealand

Testing has evolved over the years, and the industry has developed test engineering skills and practices, although not smoothly. I think we have entered an era of testing enlightenment, and there is a big shift in how organizations and testers now think of the testing role.

I observe an increasing movement toward the importance of skills. The more skills an individual has, the more valuable they become for a team or organization. Those individuals with skills that span beyond test engineering skills only are the ones that can contribute more than someone who has a basic set of test design and execution skills. This idea is emphasized by the thinking about generalizing specialists as discussed by Scott Ambler (http://www.agilemodeling.com/essays/generalizingSpecialists.htm) or T-Shaped Skills as discussed by Lisa and Janet in their books. If you want to future-proof your career, build your test engineering skills, as well as skills outside the traditional world of testing. Forget about titles; in ten years' time it is not going to mean much to anyone if you were called "test engineer," "test specialist," "tester," "test analyst," or "verification engineer." Skills are ultimately more valuable than collected job titles; I have certainly found that true in my own career.

T-shaped skills

I would look at a holistic approach characterized by inclusive "and" conversations. The best example I can think of is to combine your collection of skills in unique ways that suits your specific context, knowing that even that will change. How can you combine a set of test engineering and analysis skills in a given situation? How can you combine a set of negotiating skills with teaching skills? How can you combine different test engineering skills together to obtain better test coverage? Think "and."

I believe one of the key skills a modern practitioner must have is the ability to understand a context, understand its changing nature, and adjust accordingly. The true masters of the future workplace will be those who will be able to observe a context, apply the fit-for-purpose combination of skills, and then continually adjust the combination of skills as the context evolves. That intuition takes time to develop, and it is a constantly changing domain. Learning new skills will enrich the capability and the value that such a person brings to organizations and teams.

We bring many different skills than just test engineering skills. I would like to suggest that we consider (by unashamedly borrowing from others) a multifaceted approach. Call it the "Holistic agile testing skills" or "The ten thinking hats of agile testing," or whatever else makes sense to you. Some of these facets might be:

- **Consultant**: Yes, sometimes we will have to "consult" inside our team or with another team to help solve problems and issues.
- **Test engineering specialist**: We have to know our testing onions from shallots. We require good and solid test engineering skills.
- **Agile scholar**: Keep studying and learning about agile, bring ideas to the team, and experiment.
- **Coach**: We have great opportunities to coach the team or even co-workers (inside and outside the team). This is a life skill, in my opinion.
- **Mentor**: Sometimes we have to mentor someone in testing.
- **Facilitator**: Sometimes we just need to step into the role of facilitator for a decision, discussion, explanation, etc.
- **Change agent**: We may sometimes bring about change and upheaval, advocate a new practice/technique/method to experiment with and learn from.
- **Leader**: Yes, we may sometimes be required to step up and perform leadership in/on behalf of the team.
- **Teacher**: That goes without saying, especially if there is a shortage of testing skills in the team/organization.
- **Business domain scholar / defender of common sense / big picture thinker**: Sometimes it is good to step away and see the forest from the trees.

Lisa's and Janet's thoughts

We hope you've enjoyed reading other people's thoughts about what they consider to be a tester's role. Now we'll share ours. We've encouraged testers to help their non-tester teammates learn testing skills. When the whole team takes responsibility for quality and testing, every team member needs some grounding in testing skills. To accomplish this, we've identified skills we recommend that testing specialists should learn.

Use your thinking skills

- **collaboration skills** to participate actively in practices like mind mapping or example mapping
- **facilitation skills** to help team members communicate better, facilitate meetings such as retrospectives, facilitate workshops to help non-testers learn testing skills
- **teaching skills** to share their knowledge with other team members
- **coaching skills** to help the team identify problems and design experiments for improvements
- **communication skills** to give and receive feedback effectively (see Chapter 4, "Thinking Skills for Testing," in *More Agile Testing* for additional information)

We see a growing need for testers to act as test consultants for their teams. Many teams have a low ratio of dedicated testers to developers and other non-testing roles. We testers can add more value by helping everyone have the competencies needed to do essential testing activities. Everyone on the team will think more about testing and be more conscious of the need to build quality in from the start.

Chapter 12: Ingredients for Success

Each agile software delivery team travels its own learning journey. Our goal is to continually improve our ability to deliver value to our customers frequently, while maintaining our business's desired standard of quality. Each team is doing this with a unique combination of business domain, software product, technology stack, frameworks, and practices.

Over the years, we have found that among all these differences, certain ingredients for success benefit every team.

Success factors

In our first book, *Agile Testing*, our summary chapter comprised seven success factors we thought were necessary (although not sufficient) to be successful in delivering a quality product. It is easy to get over-whelmed by planning and executing testing activities during short delivery cycles. Below is a short list of key success factors and core agile testing practices to guide your teams.

"Whole-team approach"

Elisabeth Hendrickson taught us that "testing is an activity, not a phase." Testing is an integral part of software development, along with coding and so many other activities. With this perspective, it is easy for everyone to help with testing tasks as necessary.

Testers can teach other team members skills like eliciting concrete examples of desired and undesired behavior from business experts, evaluating different quality attributes, or doing exploratory testing.

Programmers can help testers understand the system architecture to get better testing or even teach them basic coding constructs. Each team member can transfer some of their deep skills to other team members, regardless of role.

When teams realize that testing and quality are a team problem, they can incorporate their diverse skillsets and develop an atmosphere of trust and safety, as well as create a learning environment where they can experiment and continually improve.

Drawing by Constance Hermit

Agile testing mindset

Testers are no longer the "quality police," determining "go/no-go" decisions. Testers or team members who are performing testing activities can explain the risks and impacts of test results so that the business can make an informed decision about releasing to production.

As a team member with an agile testing mindset, it means you're inquisitive and want to learn more about everything to help you do your job. It means that you apply agile principles and values. It means collaborating with the technical and business team members, keeping the big picture in mind as you put the small feature increments together. You're focused on bug prevention, so you don't have to spend so much time finding bugs later.

Drawing by Constance Hermit

Automate your regression tests

There are a few things to remember when your team starts to automate. It is a team problem, so think "whole team" and collaborate to automate at all levels. Programmers are good at writing code, testers are good at specifying tests, and people with other specialized skills on the team can help with test data, infrastructure, and more. The test automation pyramid is a good visual model to form and evolve the team's automation strategy. By keeping the tests simple and easy to maintain, a team can work toward having enough regression tests to give them confidence about releasing.

Test automation is a check to ensure that you haven't forgotten to change something, i.e., it is a change detector. A good automation strategy gives you the time to perform exploratory testing to find issues before your customer does.

Provide and obtain feedback

Successful software development depends on fast feedback. Teams need to know right away if a change has caused an unintended failure. They want to know how customers react to a new feature. Testers are central to creating and continuing to shorten the various feedback loops, including creating automated tests, engaging in exploratory testing, and observing production usage to learn how customers use the product.

People also need feedback for themselves so they can find more ways to add value. Listening and observing skills are key.

> ***Hint***: *As you collaborate with other team members, ask them what gaps you can fill and how you can contribute more effectively.*

Build a foundation of core practices

There are core practices that have proven effective in helping teams build quality into their product.

- Every team needs **continuous integration** to successfully deliver software at a frequent cadence over time. Each time a team member commits a change to the source code control repository, it should kick off a build process that integrates all code changes and verifies them with automated tests. Every team has a deployment pipeline to create a release candidate and deploy it to a test or production environment – even if it includes manual stages.
- Many teams still struggle to have reliable **test environments** that resemble production as much as possible and allow them to easily control which build version is deployed. Today's

cloud infrastructure provides even more options to create temporary test environments to test a specific build version and automatically deploy new versions to permanent test environments.

- Technical debt is like credit card debt; it continues to grow if only the minimum amount or part of the interest is paid. The technical debt continues to grow if the team doesn't take time to refactor code, create adequate automated regression tests, upgrade frameworks, and manage other necessary infrastructure. Over time even the smallest code change poses large risks and requires much time spent with manual testing tasks. Invest the time to **manage technical debt** in the code and in your automated tests.

- Small, frequent changes are generally less risky than large, infrequent ones. Less can go wrong, and failures can be quickly diagnosed. Teams that slice big feature ideas into small "**learning releases**" and even smaller stories are more likely to deliver what their customers want in a timely manner.
- **Coding and testing are part of one process.** This is the core of the whole-team approach to testing and quality. Testing and coding happen together, hand in hand, from feature idea to evaluating the feature in production.
- **Synergy between practices** comes from doing all these core practices together. Test-driven development, collective code ownership, and continuous integration ensure consistency and fast feedback. Refactoring depends on having automated

regression tests. Agile practices are tried and true and are designed to be done all together.

Collaborate with customers

Testers speak the domain language of business stakeholders and the technical language of delivery team members. Getting the right people together when a conversation is needed about how a feature should behave or how a design should look is also important. Testers can help product owners articulate business rules for each story and illustrate them with concrete examples. This is one of the most valuable ways testers contribute on teams.

Look at the big picture

While agile teams focus on small changes and small slices of features at any given time, they also need to keep the big picture in mind. Testers are talented at identifying what parts of the system might be affected by a particular small change, and they have a customer's perspective.

The agile testing quadrants model goes a long way toward helping the team keep the big picture in mind as they plan testing activities. Exploratory testing is an example of a testing activity that can uncover unexpected consequences of a new application capability. We have good ways to analyze how customers are using our product. This all helps us focus on delivering the right value.

Confidence-building practices

In our second book, *More Agile Testing*, we identified some core testing practices that help teams build the confidence needed to frequently release changes to production. These practices are especially important as more teams move toward continuous delivery or continuous deployment.

Use examples

Concrete examples of how an application capability should behave help everyone on the team understand the business rules. These examples can be turned into tests that guide development. They can be automated so the team knows when it's done with a story or feature. The automated tests become part of regression test suites that provide quick feedback on whether a new change has affected existing production behavior. Examples help teams stay on track.

Exploratory testing

Automating regression tests leaves more time for exploratory testing, one of the best ways to find the "unknown unknowns" that could cause dire production failures. Programmers can learn to do exploratory testing on each story before they deem their work "finished." This is another fast feedback loop. Everyone on the team can learn and use exploratory testing skills. They will not only identify unexpected problems but will also find missing capabilities that feed back into new feature ideas.

Feature testing

It's essential to test at all levels of detail. Because agile teams focus on the story, they need to remember to also test at the feature level. An important part of this is identifying what the feature really needs to include. Testers can help figure out what is valuable to customers by asking questions concerning what the business should drop in favor of delivering other highly valuable features.

Continual learning

Team success depends on psychological safety, trust, and time to learn. The team needs to work together to identify the biggest obstacle to delivering their desired level of quality, whether it's inadequate test automation, feedback that takes too long, or building features that nobody wanted. Then they can design small experiments to start overcoming that obstacle. Testers can help the team learn to build quality in by transferring testing skills. Other team members can help testers ramp up their T-shaped skills so they can contribute in more ways.

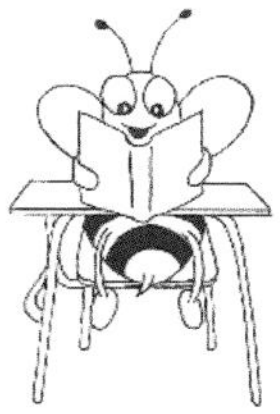

Context sensitivity

Every team is working within its unique context. The size of the company, the business domain and its regulatory environment, the technology involved, infrastructure needs – these are just some considerations for a team as it considers how to improve its ability to deliver value to customers frequently. Don't adopt a tool or practice because it's what Google or Facebook does – use what is appropriate for your context.

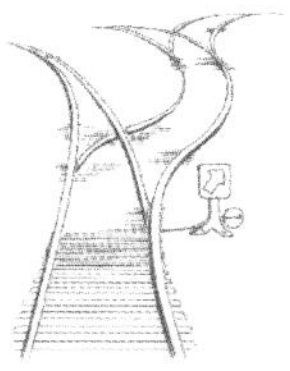

Keep it real

Testers excel at providing feedback. It can be difficult to deliver bad news. But it's important to stay grounded in reality. If a change is risky and the team hasn't adequately mitigated that risk with testing and other activities, business stakeholders need to know. Testers can act as consultants to help everyone on their team improve their testing skills and be able to make quality concerns visible to the business. When the team experiences bottlenecks with testing, make it visible, make it a team problem to solve. It can be tempting to gloss over issues to keep the business executives happy, but they won't be happy if customers experience pain.

It is also important for team morale to know they can say no. For example, "No, we can't take in any more stories," or "No, we can't add a new story unless you remove one of the others." Keep it real!

Paths to success

We know there are a lot of testers and teams out there who feel stressed, especially on teams that are still transitioning to using agile development values, principles, and practices. For example, management hasn't yet figured out how their role needs to change and may demand more frequent deliveries and impose unrealistic deadlines. The testing still must be done, and in too many cases, testers still bear total responsibility for all testing activities. We'd like to think there is some magic silver bullet tool out there that will solve all our problems, but we know that's not reality!

Turning testing problems into problems for the whole delivery team to address is vital to learning how to build quality into your products and achieving sustainable success. These key success factors and confidence-building practices provide a framework to help the team decide its next steps along a path to improvement.

In our experience, it takes years for a delivery team to achieve their desired level of performance and quality. We might add an eighth key success factor: patience! Frequent team retrospectives (we recommend at least one a week for new teams) are also key in identifying the biggest quality-related problem and designing a small experiment to start chipping away at it. The diverse skills and experience in a cross-functional team makes solving those problems much easier.

An example

The team is frustrated because the product owner rejects a high percentage of the stories they deliver. The constant re-work, sometimes days after the team thought the story was "finished," is slowing them down. Cycle time – the time from when they start working on a story to when it is deployed to production – is much longer than they'd like. What key success factor can help?

The whole-team approach is obvious. Let's get the whole team, or a representative group including all roles, together to discuss it. What confidence-building practice would help? When the product owner rejects a story, it's usually because the behavior of that part of the application is not what she wanted. The team misunderstood the requirements. The team is continually learning (one of the confidence-building practices), and one of the testers has just learned about example mapping. They decide to experiment with example mapping to see if it will build better shared understanding of each story. They hypothesize that example mapping will reduce story rejection rate by 20% over the next two weeks, resulting in a 10% savings of average cycle time.

They measure and experiment to see if their hypothesis is true. In this real example, the experiment was a success. The goals for reduction in rejection rate and cycle time were exceeded. Within two months, rejection rate and cycle time were both reduced by 50%. The team found more benefits from example mapping as it helped with specifying scenarios to guide development in the form of behavior-driven development tests. But if the experiment had failed, the team would have designed another experiment, guided by the success factors and confidence-building practices.

When our own teams feel stuck on a problem, we fall back on the key success factors and confidence-building practices, along with the ten principles for agile testing in Chapter 1, to help us plan our next steps. They will guide us along our learning journey as we improve our ability to get small, valuable changes to our customers frequently and sustainably.

Thank you for reading, and we hope you are successful in your own journey.

Glossary

Ad hoc testing: An informal testing activity where one looks for bugs in a non-structured way without any advance plan.

Context diagram: A high-level diagram that represents all external entities that may interact with a system, including other systems, environments, and activities.

Customer: Extreme programming (XP) uses the term "customer" to refer to a business stakeholder, product person, or end user who meets with the programming team to set priorities, answer questions, and make decisions about feature behavior. In contemporary agile teams, the term can represent any and all business stakeholders, product team members, end users, and anyone who helps guide development and accept delivered stories.

Endgame: The endgame is the time before release when the delivery team applies the finishing touches to the product. Not a bug-fix or "hardening" period, it is an opportunity to work with groups outside of development to help move the software into production. Examples of endgame activities include additional testing of database migrations and installation.

Iteration: Time box used for planning, with the intent that there is a "potentially shippable product" by the end. The Scrum term for this is "sprint." Planning in two-week timeframes is a common practice today, even in teams doing continuous delivery and deploying to production more often.

Kanban: A planning approach derived from Lean manufacturing in which teams work in a flow-based manner. They use work-in-progress (WIP) limits, pulling new stories in that are "ready," to fill a newly empty WIP slot. The team plans, as needed, a few new stories at a time.

Learning Release: The first release(s) delivered to a customer in order to get feedback to learn and adjust (https://medium.com/@Ardita_K/the-learning-release-70374d2450b3).

Mind map: A visual diagram used as a brainstorming tool, especially when multiple people are collaborating at once. It starts with a concept, idea, or topic in the root node, with ideas connected to the root node and to each other as they are generated. Mind maps can work well for test planning and other activities.

Pairing (pair programming, pair testing): Two people working side by side at the same workstation, preferably with two mirrored monitors, two keyboards, and two mice, to write production or test code or do other testing activities. Having two people, each with a different perspective and skill set, helps catch problems immediately and reach better solutions. In strong-style pairing, one person, the navigator, is free to observe and suggest ideas, while the other person acts as the "driver"; the driver/navigator roles switch frequently.

State Diagram: A visual technique used to give an abstract description of the **behavior**[22] of a **system**[23] in response to various events. This behavior is analyzed and represented as a series of events that can occur in one or more possible states.

Test-driven Development (TDD): In test-driven development, the programmer writes and automates a small unit test, which initially fails, before writing the minimum amount of code that will make the test pass. The code is refactored as needed to meet acceptable standards. The production code is made to work one test at a time. TDD, also known as test-driven design, is more of a code design practice than a testing activity, and helps build robust, easily maintainable code.

[22]https://en.wikipedia.org/wiki/Behavior
[23]https://en.wikipedia.org/wiki/System

Resources for Further Learning

General

Agile Testing: A Practical Guide for Testers and Agile Teams, and *More Agile Testing: Learning Journeys for the Whole Team*, Lisa Crispin and Janet Gregory, https://agiletester.ca[24]

Bibliography from *More Agile Testing*, digitized by Kristine Corbus

-https://testretreat.com/2018/01/28/more-agile-testing-introduction/

-https://testretreat.com/2018/01/29/more-agile-testing-learning-better-testing/

-https://testretreat.com/2018/01/29/more-agile-testing-planning/

-https://testretreat.com/2018/01/30/more-agile-testing-business-value

-https://testretreat.com/2018/02/15/more-agile-testing-test-automation/

Getting Shared Understanding - Collaboration

Discovery: Explore behavior using examples, Seb Rose and Gáspár Nagy, 2017, http://bddbooks.com/

User Story Mapping: Building Better Products Using Agile Software Design, Jeff Patton, O'Reilly Media, 2014.

[24]https://agiletester.ca/

Impact Mapping, Gojko Adzic, http://impactmapping.org

"Experiment with Example Mapping," https://lisacrispin.com/2016/06/02/experiment-example-mapping/

"Introduction to Example Mapping," Matt Wynne, https://cucumber.io/blog/example-mapping-introduction/

"Three Amigos Strategy," George Dinwiddie, https://www.agileconnection.com/article/three-amigos-strategy-developing-user-stories

"Our team's first mobbing session," Lisi Hocke, https://www.lisihocke.com/2017/04/our-teams-first-mobbing-session.html

"The Driver-Navigator in Strong-Style Pairing," Maaret Pyhäjärvi, https://medium.com/@maaret.pyhajarvi/the-driver-navigator-in-strong-style-pairing-2df0ecb4f657

Strong-Style Pair Programming and *Mob Programming Guidebook*, Maaret Pyhäjärvi, https://leanpub.com/u/maaretp

Exploratory Testing

Explore It: Reduce Risk and Increase Confidence with Exploratory Testing, Elisabeth Hendrickson, 2013, https://pragprog.com/book/ehxta/explore-it

Exploratory Testing, Maaret Pyhäjärvi, https://leanpub.com/exploratorytesting

DevOps, Monitoring, Observability

A Practical Guide to Testing in DevOps, Katrina Clokie, https://leanpub.com/testingindevops

"Testing in production the safe way," Cindy Sridharan, https://medium.com/@copyconstruct/testing-in-production-the-safe-way-18ca102d0ef1

"Monitoring and observability," Cindy Sridharan, https://medium.com/@copyconstruct/monitoring-and-observability-8417d1952e1c

"Charity Majors on Observability and Understanding the Operational Ramifications of a System," InfoQ interview with Charity Majors, https://www.infoq.com/articles/charity-majors-observability-failure

Google Site Reliability Engineering, https://landing.google.com/sre/

"What is Chaos Engineering[25]?" *Joe Colontonio (includes link to podcast with Tammy Butow),* https://www.joecolantonio.com/chaos-engineering/

"Tracing vs Logging vs Monitoring: What's the Difference?" Chrissy Kidd, https://www.bmc.com/blogs/monitoring-logging-tracing/

Test Automation

"Keep your automated tests simple and avoid anti-patterns," Lisa Crispin, https://www.mabl.com/blog/keep-your-automated-testing-simple

"Test automation: Five questions leading to five heuristics," Joep Shuurkes, https://testingcurve.wordpress.com/2015/03/24/test-automation-five-questions-leading-to-five-heuristics/

"Powerful test automation practices," parts 1 and 2, Lisa Crispin and Steve Vance, https://www.mabl.com/blog/powerful-test-automation-practices-pt-1, https://www.mabl.com/blog/powerful-test-automation-practices-pt-2

"Test Suite Design," Ashley Hunsberger, https://github.com/ahunsberger/testSuiteDesign

Accelerate: The Science of Lean and DevOps, Nicole Forsgren, *et al*, https://itrevolution.com/book/accelerate/

[25]https://www.joecolantonio.com/chaos-engineering/

"Analyzing automated test failures," Lisa Crispin, https://www.mabl.com/blog/lisa-webinar-analyzing-automated-ui-test-failures

"The Testing Iceberg," Seb Rose, http://claysnow.co.uk/the-testing-iceberg/

"Lower level automation and testing? Be more precise! The automation triangle revisited again!" Toyer Mamoojee, https://toyerm.wordpress.com/2018/10/16/lower-level-automation-and-testing-be-more-precise-the-automation-triangle-revisited-again

The Team Guide to Software Testability, Ash Winter and Rob Meaney, https://leanpub.com/softwaretestability

About the Authors

Janet Gregory is an agile testing coach and process consultant with DragonFire Inc. Her peers voted her as the Most Influential Agile Testing Professional Person in 2015. Janet specializes in showing agile teams how testing practices are necessary to develop good quality products. She teaches agile testing courses worldwide and enjoys spending her summers in the mountains outside Calgary.

Lisa Crispin has been spreading agile joy to the testing world and testing joy to the agile world for two decades and her peers voted her as the Most Influential Agile Testing Professional Person in 2012. Her current interests include helping teamssucceed with continuous delivery and deployment and she is a testing advocate working at mabl to explore leading practices in testing in thesoft-ware community. Lisa lives with her husband, donkeys, cats and dogs in beautiful Vermont.

Janet and Lisa are authors of *Agile Testing Condensed: A Brief Introduction* (2019), *More Agile Testing: Learning Journeys for the Whole Team* (2014), *Agile Testing: A Practical Guide for Testers and Agile Teams* (2009), the LiveLessons Agile Testing Essentials video course, and "Agile Testing for the Whole Team" 3-day training course offered through the Agile Testing Fellowship. Together, they founded the fellowship to grow a community of practitioners who care about quality.

Janet Gregory: janetgregory.ca[26] Twitter: @janetgregoryca

Lisa Crispin: lisacrispin.com[27] Twitter: @lisacrispin

Agile Testing Fellowship: agiletestingfellow.com[28] agiletester.ca[29]

[26]https://janetgregory.ca/
[27]https://lisacrispin.com/
[28]https://agiletestingfellow.com/
[29]https://agiletester.ca/

Printed in Great Britain
by Amazon

30829908R00066